WORDS FROM THE CROSS

WORDS FROM THE CROSS

Ian Hamilton

THE BANNER OF TRUTH TRUST

THE BANNER OF TRUTH TRUST

Head Office
3 Murrayfield Road
Edinburgh, EH12 6EL
UK

North America Office
PO Box 621
Carlisle, PA 17013
USA

banneroftruth.org

© Ian Hamilton 2022

*

ISBN
Print: 978 1 80040 256 0
Epub: 978 1 80040 257 7
Kindle: 978 1 80040 258 4

*

Typeset in 11/14 Adobe Garamond Pro
at The Banner of Truth Trust, Edinburgh

Printed in the USA by
Versa Press Inc.,
East Peoria, IL

To

my dear friend,

Eric J. Alexander,

encourager, example and mentor,

with my deepest affection and gratitude

CONTENTS

CHAPTER I

INTRODUCTION:
SETTING THE SCENE

THE Bible is the written revelation of God. If we did not have the Bible as 'a lamp to our feet and a light to our path' (Psa. 119:105), we would ever be wandering through this life in a mental, moral, and spiritual fog. But in his great kindness and mercy God has given us his written word. Two great themes dominate God's written revelation: (1) who he is, and (2) what he has done in his Son to save a fallen world and restore it to himself.

Within this written revelation there are certain special moments.

In Genesis 1, God introduces himself as the sovereign Creator and Lord of the cosmos.

In Genesis 15:7, God declares to Abraham, 'I am the Lord who brought you out from Ur of the Chaldeans to give you this land to possess.'

In Exodus 3:14, in response to Moses' question, 'If I come to the people of Israel and say to them, "The God of your fathers has sent me to you," and they ask me, "What is his name?" what am I to say to them?', God replied, 'I AM WHO I AM … Say this to the people of Israel, "I AM has sent me to you."'

In Isaiah 40:12-31, God tells his people that to him the nations are as a drop in the bucket and are as nothing before him. He tells them that he sits above the circle of the earth and stretches out the heavens like a curtain. He tells them that he created and names the uncountable galaxies. He tells them that he is the everlasting God, the Creator of the ends of the earth, who never wearies and whose understanding is unsearchable.

These, and other like passages, are mountain-peak moments in God's written revelation.

But none of these passages, nor all of them placed together, display God's ultimate and climactic revelation in Scripture. God most gloriously, most wonderfully, and most unfathomably reveals who he is and what he has done for this world *in the coming, living, dying and rising of his Son, Jesus Christ*. We read in John 1:18, 'No one has ever seen God; the only God [or 'Son'], who is at the Father's side, he has made him known.' Jesus is the incarnate revelation of God and his glory. In him we come face to face with the living and true God.

As the Gospel accounts of Jesus' life, death and resurrection unfold, and as the Letters of the New Testament confirm, God's revelation in his incarnate Son reaches it omega point in the cross. We read in 1 John 4:8 that 'God is love'; but immediately John continues, 'In this the love of God was made manifest among us, that God sent his only Son into the world, so that we might live through him. In this is love, not that we have loved God but that he loved us and sent his Son to be the propitiation for our sins.' The apostle John is inviting us to grasp that the essential nature of God as lover is most clearly revealed in the sin-bearing, sin-atoning, wrath-quenching death of Jesus on the cross.

The cross of Jesus Christ has always bewildered this world. In Paul's day, the preaching of the cross—the substitutionary, sin-atoning sacrifice of God's Son, Jesus Christ—was considered 'a stumbling block,' a 'scandal' and foolishness (1 Cor. 1:23). Friedrich Nietzsche, the nineteenth-century German philosopher, contemptuously dismissed Jesus as 'God on the cross' and described Christianity as 'a religion of pity,' that is, a religion to be pitied. Why? Because, he said, 'it preserves what is ripe for destruction (the weak, the poor, the downtrodden, the marginalized) and so 'thwarts the law of evolution.' Nietzsche was only saying what the world today thinks of Jesus and his cross. Yet from the beginning, Christians have gloried in the cross of Christ (1 Cor. 1:18, 22-24; 2:1, 2).

When Paul concludes his remarkable exposition of 'the gospel of God' (Rom. 1:1), he writes, 'Oh, the depths of the riches and wisdom and knowledge of God!' (Rom.

11:33). The apostle is overwhelmed and finds himself out of his depth as he expounds the multifaceted glory of the cross-work of the Lord Jesus Christ. The message of the cross is unimaginably rich and glorious, but it is also beyond our fathoming. It is a bottomless deep. Charles Wesley expressed it well when he wrote,

'Tis mystery all! The Immortal dies:
Who can explore his strange design.[1]

We can never approach the cross of Christ dispassionately, far less clinically. We must ever approach Calvary with bated breath, with awe and wonder, with holy trepidation. This is why for the apostle Paul the preaching of the cross was the fundamental pulse beat of his ministry. He told the Corinthian church, which was so impressed with the sophisticated but empty rhetoric of certain teachers, 'when I came to you, brothers, I did not come proclaiming to you the testimony of God with lofty speech or wisdom. For I decided to know nothing among you except Jesus Christ and him crucified' (1 Cor. 2:1, 2). For the early church, the cross of Christ was the centrepiece and glory of its gospel message. It is not surprising then to find Paul saying, 'far be it from me to boast except in the cross of our Lord Jesus Christ, by which the world has been crucified to me, and I to the world' (Gal. 6:14). The cross is the Christian's great and only boast because on the cross God was reconciling lost, judgment-deserving

[1] From the hymn 'And Can It Be' by Charles Wesley.

sinners to himself through the substitutionary atoning sacrifice of his Son (2 Cor. 5:18-21).

During the past two thousand years, many fine books have been written on the meaning and significance of the death of Jesus Christ. In the fourth century, Athanasius wrote, *The Incarnation of the Word of God* (*De Incarnatione Verbi Dei*). At the end of the eleventh century, Anselm wrote, *Why God Became Man* (*Cur Deus Homo*). During the Reformation, most of the magisterial Reformers wrote on the saving nature of Christ's death on the cross. John Calvin's exposition of the atonement in *The Institutes of the Christian Religion* stands out for its clarity, richness, and evangelical warmth. In the more recent past, two books stand out (at least for me): Hugh Martin's *The Atonement*, and John Murray's, *Redemption, Accomplished and Applied*. When I first read Murray as a young Christian, I had no idea how rich and profound was the meaning and significance of the death of Christ.

The aim of this little book is to stand on the shoulders of these giants of the faith, and to provide a perspective of the atonement from the lips of the Saviour himself. Jesus knew why he had come into the world; he had come 'to give his life a ransom for many' (Mark 10:45). He understood that his mission was to bring life in all its fullness to a world in rebellion against God (John 10:10). As the shadow of the cross began to penetrate his human soul, Jesus exclaimed, 'Truly, truly, I say to you, unless a grain of wheat falls into the earth and dies, it remains alone; but if it dies, it bears much fruit' (John 12:24). As he expired on the cross he said, 'It is finished' (John 19:30). The work entrusted to him by his Father in times eternal, the work of becoming a saving, sin-atoning sacrifice for a lost world, had been completed. He then bowed his head and dismissed his spirit (John 19:30).

CHAPTER 2

THE PROMISED SAVIOUR

To appreciate the significance of Jesus' words from the cross, we must see them in the light of the Old Testament's foretelling of Jesus' coming as the long-promised Saviour, the Servant of the Lord who would triumph over Satan and undo the tragedy of Adam's sin.

Amidst the wreckage of Adam and Eve's rebellion in the Garden of Eden, God made a promise. He addressed Satan, who, in the guise of a serpent, had deceived and seduced the first man and women into their rebellion: 'I will put enmity between you and the woman, and between your offspring and her offspring; he shall bruise your head, and you shall bruise his heel' (Gen. 3:15). From that epochal moment, God's people on earth waited for and wondered who that 'offspring,' that 'he,' would be. They knew he would be the offspring or seed of the woman, he would not be an angel. As the years and ages passed, the people of God must have longed for the coming of this 'offspring.' They must have wondered how he would be recognized. Would he come with pomp and circumstance? Would he come in stately splendour to vanquish the enemy, and the enemies of God's people with overwhelming power?

As the Old Testament develops, slowly, very slowly, we are introduced to the one who will crush the serpent's head. We are told that he would come from the family of Abraham (see Gen. 12:3). We discover he would come from the tribe of Judah (see Gen. 49:10). As the history of redemption unfolds, we further learn that he would be a greater prophet than Moses (see Deut. 18:15-19). Then we are told that he would come from the line of David. Remarkably, through Isaiah the prophet, we are told that he will be born of a virgin (Isa. 7:14), that his name will called, 'Wonderful Counsellor, Mighty God, Everlasting Father, Prince of Peace.' Isaiah continues, 'Of the increase of his government and of peace there will be no end, on the throne of David and over his kingdom, to establish it and to uphold it with justice and with righteousness from this time forth and forevermore' (Isa. 9:6). As the portrait of the promised Deliverer continues to develop, we discover that he would be born in Bethlehem and that he would rule Israel, 'whose coming forth is from of old, from ancient days' (Mic. 5:2). It is as if we are looking at a picture that is slowly being painted, or watching a film negative being developed. But the question still hung in the air, Who is he? How will we recognize him?

It is in the prophecy of Isaiah that the portrait of the promised Messiah reaches new heights of clarity. In four passages—four songs or poems celebrating the coming Messiah—God paints us a picture of the one he calls 'my servant, my chosen one' (Isa. 42:1). This designation is deeply suggestive. Here is the Servant of God who will triumph where Adam failed. Here is the better Son than Adam (see Luke 3:38) who will crush the serpent's head. We know these songs are speaking about Jesus from the testimony of the New Testament (Matt. 12:15-21; Acts 8:32-35).

It is, therefore, as the Servant of the Lord that Jesus speaks his words of dying love and grace from the cross. To better appreciate the words Jesus spoke, we need first to reflect on the Servant of whom these songs in Isaiah's prophecy speak.

CHAPTER 3

THE SAVIOUR'S FIRST SONG

Isaiah 42:1-4

THE opening word of chapter 42 is significant,
'*Behold*.' It is the third in a triad of 'Beholds' (see
41:24, 29). Now, God says to his people as they
contemplate the as yet unimaginable prospect of exile,
'Behold my servant.' The first two 'Beholds' call God's
people to consider the futility of idols and idolatry. Now,
the Lord says, 'Behold my Servant, my answer to the
futility, idolatry, ignorance, and tragedy of this world.'

In this first of the Servant Songs we are introduced
to God's unique, world-transforming Servant. A word
portrait of this Servant is begun that will reach its remarkable climax in the fourth and final Servant Song in Isaiah
chapter 53. We are told a number of things about this
Servant:

First, he is *God's servant*. The Lord God calls him
'my servant.' This Servant was not the first to be called

'my servant.' God calls Moses 'my servant' (Num. 12:7; Josh. 1:2). But of no servant does God say, 'my chosen, in whom my soul delights' (Isa. 42:1). It is these words that are echoed at Jesus' baptism (Matt. 3:17) and again at his transfiguration (Matt. 17:5). It is as the Servant of the Lord that Jesus came in obedience to the will of his Father (John 6:38), to crush the serpent and to set free his captives. God's first servant-son failed disastrously in the Garden of Eden; God's beloved and well-pleasing Servant-Son would be 'obedient to the point of death, even death on a cross' (Phil. 2:8).

Second, he is *God's dependent servant.* The dependent nature of this servant's life is highlighted: God himself will 'uphold' him. God says 'I will put my Spirit upon him.' In his life of service to the Lord, the Servant will not act autonomously. He will live out his life of service upheld by God and enabled by the Spirit of God. It is this truth that lies behind Jesus' words, 'I can do nothing by myself' (John 5:30).

Third, he will be *God's undeviatingly faithful servant.* We are told 'he will bring forth justice to the nations (Isa. 42:1) and 'he will not grow faint or be discouraged till he has established justice in the earth' (verse 4). Unlike Adam, this servant will not fail, he will not falter, he will not give up, he will not turn back, but he will fulfil the work entrusted to him by his Father. This note of absolute faithfulness not only describes the promised Messiah, it also becomes one of the hallmarks of authentic servant ministry in the Messiah's church, 'it is required of stewards that they be found faithful' (1 Cor. 4:2).

Fourth, he will *not be an aggressive or self-advertising servant*: 'He will not cry aloud or lift up his voice, or make it heard in the street' (Isa. 42:3). The point of the verbs is not that he will not preach in the open air, but that he will not be self-promoting. The Lord's Servant will be humble and self-effacing. He will never say arrogantly in word or attitude, 'Look at me.' It is remarkable that on the only occasion when Jesus drew attention to his character he said, 'learn from me, for I am gentle and lowly in heart' (Matt. 11:29).

Fifth, he will be a *gentle and tender-hearted servant*: 'a bruised reed he will not break, and a faintly burning wick he will not quench' (Isa. 42:3). No trembling, fearful, broken sinner need fear to come to him. This Servant knows that we are all 'damaged goods.' But he is rich in mercy and full of grace (John 1:14). Earlier in chapter 40, Isaiah beautifully pictured the tender-heartedness of 'the arm of the Lord' (a phrase that describes the Lord's Servant (see Isa. 53:1), 'He will tend his flock like a shepherd; he will gather the lambs in his arms; he will carry them in his bosom, and gently lead those that are with young' (40:11). This is the Lord's Servant.

In his letter to the church in Philippi Paul summons God's people to cultivate the servant-mindedness of the Lord Jesus Christ. He is first our Saviour and King, but he is also our example (1 Pet. 2:21-23; Phil. 2:5-8).

It is worth pausing to ask, Does this begin to describe me? If you are a pastor, an elder, a deacon, does this describe you? Jesus said, 'I am among you as the one who serves' (Luke 22:27). And this Servant was none other than the Lord of glory, the only begotten of the Father, God the Son.

CHAPTER 4

THE SAVIOUR'S SECOND SONG

Isaiah 49:1-7

THE first Song outlined the character, the temperament, the faithfulness, the remarkable tenderness of the Lord's Servant, God's answer to the emptiness, the bleakness, the futility, and the fallenness of this world.

In this second Song, the divinely painted portrait of God's 'serpent crusher' is further developed. There are two sections:

(1) Verses 1-5: the Servant himself speaks.
(2) Verses 6, 7: the Servant's Lord speaks.

(1) *The Servant speaks* (ver. 1-5). There is something both unexpected and yet wonderful in what the Servant speaks. Again the summons in verse 1, as in 42:1, is for us to 'give attention'; something momentous is about to

happen. We could translate, 'Be all ears,' 'Take care how you hear.' Unlike the first Song, we now have autobiography. The Servant knows that he is the Lord's Servant. He knows he has been chosen from before he was born. He knows he has been wonderfully gifted with a 'mouth like a sharp sword.' He knows he is uniquely special (verse 2b, 3). He has been prepared for over thirty years, but for what? to be equipped to be our Saviour, the serpent crusher. In him the Lord will 'display his beauty' (reflect on Isa. 53:1).

The question needs to be asked, Why is he called 'Israel' here (Isa. 49:3)? Because he represents all of God's people; he stands before God in our place, as our covenant head.

Moreover, he knows that he is highly honoured by the Lord (verse 5). There is so much the Servant knows.

Now read verse 4a, 'But I said, "I have laboured in vain; I have spent my strength for nothing and vanity.' Were you expecting this? God's unique Servant, his serpent crusher, his Messiah, his own Son, yet look at what he is saying!

What are we to make of this? Can this be sinful despondency? Absolutely not! Here we see the true, holy humanity of our Saviour. His humanity was not a charade. His humanity was a true humanity, and being a true humanity it could not be omniscient. It cost our Lord Jesus to stand before God in our place. He did not cruise effortlessly to glory.

Think of these statements we read in the Gospels: 'How long am I to be with you? How long am I to bear with you' (Matt. 17:17). 'O you of little faith' (Matt. 8:26) 'You will leave me alone' (John 16:32). As he hung on Calvary's cross, there was no reassuring voice from heaven. Absolute silence! Impenetrable darkness! Unimaginable suffering! Is it any wonder that the God-Man cried, 'My God, my God, Why have you forsaken me?' If Jesus had not cried 'Why?', his humanity would have been a fraud. Everything seemed a failure. This is why we must focus on the 'My God, my God.'

And here in the first part of verse 4 of Isaiah 49 we must see the cry of despair in the light of the affirmation of faith in the second part of the same verse. What did God's Servant do when utter darkness covered his soul? Did he despair? Did he renounce God? Did he abandon his calling as the Lord's serpent crusher? No! 'Yet surely my right is with the Lord, and my recompense with my God.' Here is the Lord's Servant and in his human extremity he continues to trust his God. All the lights have gone out, but faith in God remained unbowed. Nowhere did faith in God shine more brightly than in Jesus' cry of forsakenness.

(2) *The Servant's Lord speaks* (verses 6, 7). The Lord's response to his Servant's desolation is to tell him of the universal significance of his suffering: 'I will make you as a light for the nations, that my salvation may reach to

the end of the earth. Thus says the Lord, the Redeemer of Israel and his Holy One, to one deeply despised, abhorred by the nation, the servant of rulers: "Kings shall see and arise; princes, and they shall prostrate themselves; because of the Lord, who is faithful, the Holy One of Israel, who has chosen you"' (read Acts 13:47). The Lord is telling his Servant, his own Son, that his life and mission will not end in defeat or despair. He will be 'despised and rejected by men' (Isa. 53:3), but kings and princes will prostrate themselves before him. How will this happen? Notice the concluding words of verse 7, 'because of the Lord, who is faithful, the Holy One of Israel, who has chosen you.' In other words, God promises that he himself will see to it (read the concluding words of Isa. 9:7).

This second Song highlights the true humanity of the Servant and the universal significance of his life and mission. Where Adam failed and where the Jews as a people failed to be God's faithful servants, Jesus would triumph.

So, what are we to take to heart from this second Song?

We see, first, the cost to the Lord Jesus Christ of becoming a light to the nations. The great salvation Jesus won for us cost him dearly. Our redemption was won at a cost we will never fathom. The holy pathos of verse 4 is deeply moving—and it was all for us.

Second, the suffering endured by our Saviour should bring huge encouragement to us in the midst of the trials and sorrows of this life. When sorrows overwhelm you and life seems utterly bleak, remember that your God is at work, fulfilling his eternal purpose in your life, just as he was in the life of your Saviour. Your tears and sorrows are not meaningless! (Rom. 8:28; Gen. 50:20). Do you think that your life has amounted to nothing? When you look at yourself, what do you see? Failure? Are you tempted to think, 'I have amounted to nothing'? God was at work in the darkness that enshrouded Jesus' life. In the midst of the seeming failures God was doing a work that no one could see, or would believe if told. Who looking at the cross would have said, 'Wonder of wonders!

> Love so amazing, so divine,
> Demands my soul, my life my all'?[1]

Who would have thought looking at the bleeding, expiring Jesus of Nazareth, 'God is in Christ reconciling the world to himself'? But he was. In your darkness and despondency, 'Trust in the Lord' (read Isa. 50:10).

---

[1] From the hymn 'When I Survey the Wondrous Cross' by Isaac Watts.

CHAPTER 5

THE SAVIOUR'S THIRD SONG

Isaiah 50:4-11

THE third Servant Song continues to add to the picture of the promised Messiah, the serpent crusher. The Jews were looking for a king like the other kings that strutted about the ancient Near East, but God had another kind of king to give to his people, a king like no other. God is always turning the values and expectations of the world upside down. God's king would be a deeply despised king (Isa. 49:7), but a king in whom God himself delighted (42:1), a king who would obey God perfectly, who would, unlike Adam, be faithful unto death and beyond.

The Servant's Education

The opening verses picture a dark scene. God has cast off his people and the reason is stated plainly (verse 1b). Verse 2 begins with God plaintively asking, 'Why, when I came, was there no man; why, when I called, was there no one to answer?' But God had another man untouched by Adam's sin, a man 'holy, innocent, unstained, separated from sinners' (Heb. 7:26). This man would undo Adam's tragedy and fulfil all righteousness.

The Song begins by highlighting the education the Servant received. God's Servant had been given a mission, to minister God's grace to the weary and heavy laden, to help the burdened and overwhelmed (42:3). He was to be a physician of souls and his medicine was to be the word of God. In his earthly life, Jesus did this with insight and understanding, with gentleness and compassion. The question I would like us to ask is, 'How did he become such a physician of souls? How did he know the Scriptures so well?' The answer this Song gives is perhaps surprising: his understanding did not come to him easily or effortlessly. Isaiah writes, 'Morning by morning he awakens; he awakens my ear to hear as those who are taught.'

'The Lord God has opened my ear, and I was not rebellious; I turned not backward.' Our Lord Jesus' humanity was not a charade. The Son of God in our flesh was not excused the educative process of learning. Morning by morning, day by day, he applied himself to hearing, reading, pondering, memorizing the written word of God. There were no supernatural shortcuts to understanding. There was no co-mingling of his humanity and deity. The writer to the Hebrews tells us 'He learned obedience' (Heb. 5:8). In his Gospel, Luke tells us that Jesus 'increased in wisdom and in stature and in favour with God and man' (Luke 2:52). Our Saviour knew from experience that there are 'No gains without pains.'

For the first thirty or so years of his life, Jesus developed mentally, emotionally, physically, and spiritually. The maturative and educative processes of ordinary humanity were his daily experience. When Satan tempted him in the wilderness, Jesus was able effortlessly to bring words from Deuteronomy immediately to mind (see Matt. 4:1-11). He did not have a Bible in his pocket. There was no Bible concordance to hand. How did he know those so appropriate texts? He had learned them and memorized them. This Servant was truly human. His divine nature existed mysteriously with his human nature, but without any confusion, mixture, or division.

Reading God's word daily, taking its truth to heart, meditating on its truth, and memorizing its words are a necessary part of the believing life. Fitness for useful service in God's kingdom will follow and imitate the pattern first etched in the life of the Lord Jesus Christ.

The Servant's Suffering

This third Song continues to highlight the suffering the Servant experienced. Once again the developing portrait reveals the dark colours of suffering: 'I gave my back to those who strike, and my cheeks to those who pull out the beard; I hid not my face from disgrace and spitting' (verse 6). The Son of God lived out his servanthood undaunted by the sufferings that increasingly engulfed him—though the sufferings were costly to him. For Christians it is vital we understand that union with Christ inevitably means union with him in his sufferings. As it was with the Master, so it will be with his servants (see John 15:18-20). The Lord did not hide from his disciples, and does not hide from us, the cost of faithfulness.

The reasons why Jesus suffered are not hard to find. He was not bad, or difficult, or divisive, or blasphemous. On the contrary, he was incarnate goodness. He spoke truth in a world of lies. He punctured pride and arrogance. He exposed religious hypocrisy. But there was something deeper at work. This 'something deeper' is developed most remarkably, as we will see, in the fourth of the Servant Songs.

The Servant's Help

In verses 7-9 we are told of the help the Lord's Servant was given as he faithfully and undauntedly fulfilled his calling and mission. Twice, in verse 7 and again in verse 9, the Servant declares, 'the Lord God helps me.' Earlier in the first Song (Isa. 42:1), the Lord God promised to 'uphold' his Servant and to put his Spirit upon him. In his mission the Lord's Servant will be given the enabling, upholding help of the Lord's Spirit. This is a truth the New Testament impresses upon us. As Jesus began his public ministry, he submitted himself to John's baptism, identifying himself with the sinful humanity he had come to save. As he did so, 'immediately he went up from the water, and behold, the heavens were opened to him, and he saw the Spirit of God descending like a dove and coming to rest on him; and behold, a voice from heaven said, "This is my beloved Son, with whom I am well pleased"' (Matt. 3:16, 17), words that more than echo Isaiah 42:1.

Throughout his ministry and mission, Jesus was supported by the help of his 'best friend,' the Holy Spirit. This upholding help reached its climax on the cross when he 'through the eternal Spirit offered himself without blemish to God' (Heb. 9:14). It is this same Holy Spirit who is the ever-present, indwelling helper of believers as we live as pilgrims and strangers in this fallen world (Rom. 8:26). As with our Lord Jesus, the Holy Spirit is ever present to help us fight the good fight of the faith, to resist and refuse the temptations of Satan, and finally enter the glory of God's nearer presence (Heb. 4:15).

The closing verses of the Song (Isa. 50:10, 11), are a plea for us to follow the Servant.

Perhaps you are thinking, 'What does all this mean for me as I raise children, work 9 to 5, struggle with ill health, face disappointments, lose people I love?' Listen to what God's Servant-Messiah says (verse 10). There are two ways to live: You can live in the light of verse 10, trusting the Lord, his character, his promises, his Son; or in the light of verse 11, trusting your own judgment, living 'by the light of your own fire.' Two ways to live. 'Choose this day whom you will serve' (Josh. 24:15).

CHAPTER 6

THE SAVIOUR'S FOURTH SONG

Isaiah 52:13–53:12

O CTAVIUS WINSLOW (1808–78) memorably wrote, 'Who delivered up Jesus to die? Not Judas for money; not the Jews for envy; not Pilate for fear; but the Father for love.' This is precisely how the New Testament understands the death of Jesus: 'This Jesus, delivered up according to the definite plan and foreknowledge of God, you crucified and killed by the hands of lawless men (Acts 2:23). Judas, the Jews, and Pilate all conspired, they were all guilty; but the one ultimately responsible for delivering up Jesus to the cursed death of the cross was his Father. The question that must be answered is, Why?

No passage in the Bible more clearly explains this 'Why?' than the fourth Servant Song.

Isaiah has painted for us a developing portrait of God's Servant, the one who would crush the serpent and bring salvation in all its fullness to this world. Isaiah has highlighted his gentleness, his faithfulness, his fragile humanity, his unflinching resolve not to turn back, the beginning of his suffering. Now it is as if he unveils the portrait and says, 'Behold your Saviour!' It is a remarkable and completely surprising description. What were God's people waiting for, what had God promised them? A Messiah, a serpent crusher, a deliverer. What does Isaiah picture for us? A despised, utterly unattractive, rejected man, a seemingly helpless victim of evil-hearted men (verse 1, 2, 7-9), a lamb led to the slaughter, innocent but condemned. 'This is your Messiah. The serpent crusher. The rescuer.'

It seemed bizarre to the ancient world—Jews and Gentiles alike—that Christians believed in a despised, rejected, crucified Saviour (1 Cor. 1:22, 23). Who in their right mind would put their hope for time and eternity in a crucified Messiah?

This is what Isaiah 53 explains, perhaps more vividly than anywhere else in the Bible. Isaiah was writing over seven hundred years before Jesus' birth and yet his portrait of God's Suffering Servant perfectly foretold the whole course of his life from womb to tomb. There are three notes we should especially consider in this Song.

First, the Song explains why someone so innocent (verse 9a), was 'stricken,' 'afflicted,' 'pierced,' and 'crushed.'

> He was pierced for our transgressions; he was crushed
> for our iniquities; upon him was the chastisement that

brought us peace, and with his wounds we are healed. All we like sheep have gone astray; we have turned—every one—to his own way; and the Lord has laid on him the iniquity of us all (ver. 5, 6).

It was 'for our transgressions,' 'for our iniquities,' that he suffered. On him the Lord laid the 'iniquity of us all.' Here, perhaps as nowhere else, we are presented with three foundational truths regarding Christ's atonement:

Substitution, he was there taking our place;

Imputation, God imputed, reckoned to him our sin (2 Cor. 5:21);

Covenant headship, he was there as our covenant head, assuming to himself, righteously as well as graciously, our liabilities before a holy God.

This is why Christians glory in the cross of Christ (Gal. 6:14). This is why we boast in a crucified Messiah.

Second, in verse 10a the Song remarkably answers the question, Who delivered up Jesus to die? Ultimately it was not the Jews for envy or Judas for money or Pilate for fear; it was the Father for love: 'it was the will of the Lord to crush him; he has put him to grief.' This is the amazing truth the New Testament highlights (read John 3:16; 1 John 4:10). Out of his great love for his world, God spared not his only Son (Rom. 8:32). Jesus did not die to win us the Father's love, he died as the provision of the Father's love for us. The hymn writer captures this truth memorably:

Here is love, vast as the ocean
  Loving kindness as the flood
When the Prince of Life, our Ransom
  Shed for us His precious blood
Who His love will not remember?
  Who can cease to sing His praise?
He can never be forgotten
  Throughout Heaven's eternal days

On the mount of crucifixion
  Fountains opened deep and wide
Through the floodgates of God's mercy
  Flowed a vast and gracious tide
Grace and love, like mighty rivers
  Poured incessant from above
And Heaven's peace and perfect justice
  Kissed a guilty world in love.[1]

Third, in Isaiah 52:13-15 and 53:11, 12, the Song highlights the Servant's triumph and exaltation:

Behold, my servant shall act wisely; he shall be high and lifted up, and shall be exalted … Kings shall shut their mouths because of him, for that which has not been told them they see, and that which they have not heard they understand. … Therefore I will divide him a portion with the many, and he shall divide the spoil with the strong, because he poured out his soul to death and was numbered with the transgressors; yet

---

[1] A Welsh hymn written by William Rees and translated by William Edwards.

he bore the sin of many, and makes intercession for the transgressors.

God's ultimate purpose in delivering up his Son was not our salvation but his exaltation (read Psa. 2; Phil. 2:9-11). Our salvation and adoption is God's '*proximate* purpose,' the exaltation of his Son as 'the firstborn of many brothers' (Rom. 8:29), is God's *ultimate* purpose.

It is this Servant who speaks from the cross. It was Augustine who wrote that the cross was 'the pulpit of God's love.' Here as nowhere else, 'God shows [or demonstrates] his love for us in that while we were still sinners, Christ died for us' (Rom. 5:8). To the cross of Christ we now turn.

CHAPTER 7

THE SHADOW OF THE CROSS: JESUS IN GETHSEMANE

A CURSORY reading of the Gospel narratives of Jesus' arrest, trial, and crucifixion, could give the impression that Jesus was caught up in a conspiracy from which he was helpless to free himself. One of his own disciples, Judas, betrays him. One of his closest disciples, Peter, denies him three times. All of his disciples desert him and leave him to face the ignominy and brutality alone. It can hardly be denied that Jesus' enemies, the Jewish religious leaders, were succeeding in their long-devised plot to kill Jesus. But behind the Jews' plotting, Peter's denials, Judas' betrayal, and the disciples' desertion, a deeper, divine reality was at work. Jesus is where he is, not because wicked men have conspired against him, cornered him, and have him in their power. Jesus is where he is by 'the definite plan and foreknowledge of God' (Acts 2:23).

Jesus himself is deeply conscious that his times are in higher hands:

> The Son of Man goes as it is written of him (Matt. 26 24);
>
> Do you think that I cannot appeal to my Father, and he will at once send me more than twelve legions of angels? But how then should the Scriptures be fulfilled, that it must be so? (Matt. 26:53, 54);
>
> You would have no authority over me at all unless it had been given you from above (John 19:11).

Jesus is no helpless pawn in a dark tragedy; he is submitting in loving obedience to the will of his heavenly Father. He is self-consciously aware of the divine drama that is being orchestrated in and around his life. It is a majestic, purposeful Jesus Christ who dominates the landscape of this drama. He is not cowering in fearful terror. Jesus is living under the royal, wise, sovereign, saving purpose of his Father. He is marching in believing obedience to the will of the heavenly Father (John 6:38).

It should not be thought, however, that Jesus marched relentlessly forward to the cross with a calm, unperturbed soul. The crisis of Gethsemane was a genuine, soul-wrenching crisis for the Son of God. As the shadow of the cross began to fall across and penetrate his human soul, Jesus 'began to be sorrowful and troubled' (Matt. 26:37). He said to Peter, James and John, 'My soul is very sorrowful, even to death.' As Jesus contemplated all that lay before him, he 'fell on his face and prayed … "My Father, if it is possible, let this cup pass from me, nevertheless, not as I will, but as you will"' (Matt. 26:39). There was nothing effortless, far less contrived, about Jesus' felt agony. In dramatic contrast to the first man, Adam, who capitulated in a garden, God's last Adam and second man (see 1 Cor. 15:45, 47), resisted the temptation to capitulate in another garden. In his human agony of soul, Jesus said, 'nevertheless, not as I will, but as you will.'

If Jesus had not prayed, 'My Father, if it be possible, let this cup pass from me,' his true humanity would have been in question. How could holy, sinless humanity face the awful prospect of drinking the cup of God's wrath, and not shrink from the drinking? How could the one who was face to face with God in the beginning (John 1:1), and who was the Father's beloved Son, not ask for the cup of damnation to pass from him, if this would be in harmony with his Father's will?

It is Jesus' experience in Gethsemane that helps prepare us for unimaginable agony, physical but above all spiritual, that will consume him on Calvary's cross. It is Gethsemane that shows us a holy, humble, obediently resolved Jesus, embracing the will of his Father that would make him who had no sin, to be sin for us, so that in him we might become the righteousness of God (see 2 Cor. 5:21).

CHAPTER 8

THE SUFFERINGS OF THE SERVANT PROPHESIED[1]

THE Old Testament Scriptures anticipated the intense sufferings of God's Messiah. Before we consider Jesus' seven words from the cross, it will be helpful to reflect on the deep personal anguish of the Messiah as he faces the agony of the cross. This deep aguish is etched in the boldest of language in three psalms—69, 22, and 40. In them we find God's Messiah praying, pleading for the sustaining help of God as he bears the weight of his people's sins and endures in their place God's holy and just wrath.

In Psalm 69 we hear God's suffering Servant crying out for God's support and strength as he finds himself

---

[1] The chapter, 'Gethsemane: The Agony of Prayer,' in Hugh Martin's *The Shadow of Calvary* (Edinburgh: Banner of Truth Trust, 2016) is a moving and insightful exposition of the agony experienced by God's Servant-Son, Jesus Christ.

about to be overwhelmed by 'deep waters':

> Save me, O God! For the waters have come up to my neck. I sink in deep mire, where there is no foothold; I have come into deep waters, and the flood sweeps over me. I am weary with my crying out; my throat is parched. My eyes grow dim with waiting for my God ... O God, you know my folly; the wrongs I have done are not hidden from you. Let not those who hope in you be put to shame through me, O Lord GOD of hosts; let not those who seek you be brought to dishonour through me, O God of Israel ... Deliver me from sinking in the mire; let me be delivered from my enemies and from the deep waters. Let not the flood sweep over me, or the deep swallow me up, or the pit close its mouth over me ... Reproaches have broken my heart, so that I am in despair. I looked for pity, but there was none, and for comforters, but I found none. They gave me poison for food, and for my thirst they gave me sour wine to drink.

There is a startling boldness and even unexpectedness about this suffering Servant's cries. How are we to understand, 'you know my folly; the wrongs I have done are not hidden from you'? The most insightful commentary on these startling words is 2 Cor. 5:21, 'For our sake he made him to be sin who knew no sin, so that in him we might become the righteousness of God.' It is as the Substitute of sinners that the Servant is suffering.[1]

---

[1] Hugh Martin, *Shadow of Calvary*, p. 44.

The same anguished cries are found in Psalm 22:

> My God, my God, why have you forsaken me? Why
> are you so far from saving me, from the words of my
> groaning? O my God, I cry by day, but you do not
> answer, and by night, but I find no rest … All who
> see me mock me; they make mouths at me; they wag
> their heads; 'He trusts in the Lord; let him deliver him;
> let him rescue him, for he delights in him!' Be not far
> from me, for trouble is near, and there is none to help
> … I am poured out like water, all my bones are out
> of joint; my heart is like wax; it is melted within my
> breast; my strength is dried up like a potsherd, and
> my tongue sticks to my jaws; you lay me in the dust
> of death. For dogs encompass me; a company of evil-
> doers encircles me; they have pierced my hands and
> feet—I can count all my bones—they stare and gloat
> over me; they divide my garments among them, and
> for my clothing they cast lots. But you, O Lord, do
> not be far off! O you my help, come quickly to my aid!
> Deliver my soul from the sword, my precious life from
> the power of the dog!

A similar, even identical, pathology is seen in Psalm
40:

> For evils have encompassed me beyond number; my
> iniquities have overtaken me, and I cannot see; they
> are more than the hairs of my head; my heart fails me.
> Be pleased, O Lord, to deliver me! O Lord, make haste
> to help me!

Hugh Martin sums up the united witness of the three psalms:

> In these supplications the one unvarying object of desire is divine help, preservation, grace that he may victoriously do and suffer the whole will of God. His crushing anxiety is that he may not fail nor waver from his obedience till he shall have done all that will of God on account of which a body was prepared for him.[1]

As he contemplated the as yet wholly unimaginable suffering that awaited him, Jesus prayed, 'My Father, if this [cup] cannot pass unless I drink it, your will be done' (Matt. 26:42). Come what may, Jesus had come not to do his own will, but the will of the Father who sent him (John 6:38).

[1] Hugh Martin, *Shadow of Calvary*, p. 43.

CHAPTER 9

JESUS' ARREST AND TRIAL

As the four Gospels unfold, and as Jesus' enemies relentlessly plot his demise, Jesus faces his approaching destiny with calmness and resolve. He knows that 'the hour' decreed from times eternal for him to be offered up as an atoning sacrifice for sin will soon dawn (John 12:27). He has forewarned his disciples that 'the Son of Man will be delivered over to the chief priests and the scribes, and they will condemn him to death and deliver him over to the Gentiles. And they will mock him and spit on him, and flog him and kill him. And after three days he will rise' (Mark 10:33, 34). Although he cannot yet fully grasp the suffering that will engulf him, Jesus knows that the path that lies before him will consume him. His soul, he told Peter, James and John, was 'very sorrowful, even to death' (Mark 14:34). But nothing will be allowed to deflect him from his 'obedience unto death' (Phil. 2:8).

The days immediately prior to Jesus' death on the cross were preceded by his betrayal by Judas his disciple, his arrest at the behest of the Jews, and his trial before Pilate the Roman governor. Each of the Gospels highlights the wickedness and perversity of the events that have brought Jesus to Pilate's judgment hall. But what stands out in the narrative is not the evil that animates Jesus' religious enemies, rather it is the calmness and silence that Jesus exhibits that dominates every scene.

CHAPTER 10

DYING WORDS

As Jesus hung on the cross, he uttered seven words or sayings. There may or may not be significance in the number 'seven.' In the Bible *seven* represents completeness (think of the letters to the seven churches in Rev. 2, 3). There is, however, huge significance in the actual words that Jesus spoke (sometimes cried out) as he hung on Calvary's cross, bearing the sin and divine judgment on that sin for a world of lost sinners.

Any man's dying words are significant. This dying man was none other than the God-Man, the eternal Son of God who became flesh (John 1:14) and he died 'the righteous for the unrighteous, that he might bring us to God' (1 Pet. 3:18). Surely his dying words deserve our highest interest and most thoughtful enquiry.

The cross is the ultimate and most intimate revelation of God. On a garbage heap, outside the city of Jerusalem, the Lord of glory was crucified between two thieves.

And yet the apostle John could write, 'we have seen his glory, glory as of the only Son from the Father, full of grace and truth' (John 1:14)—the glory of God revealed, even displayed, in a life despised and rejected by men (Isa. 53:3)!—the glory of God revealed and displayed, in a bloodied, nail-pierced, spat upon, mocked and humiliated man! This all seems so unbelievable, especially when we grasp that Jesus is where he is, not because Judas betrayed him, not because the Jews conspired against him, not because Pilate in fear condemned him, but because the Father in love for us delivered him up (Acts 2:23, 24; Rom. 8:32).

But now he is hanging nailed and bloodied on a Roman cross. His disciples have abandoned him and soon he will experience the abandonment of his Father. Soldiers are mocking him, spitting on him, reviling him. What happens next is a series of statements from the lips of the crucified, abandoned, bloodied but obedient Son of God. Each of Jesus' seven statements from the cross give us a revealing insight into the character and nature of God. Here is a 'theology of the cross' from the lips of the Crucified One.

The Obedient Son

In the Old Testament, the hope that God held out to his covenant people (Isa. 49:6a) and to all the nations of the world (Isa. 49:6b), was particularly focused on his Servant. In the latter chapters of Isaiah, we are given an increasingly detailed word picture of this Servant. As we have seen, in the four Servant Songs (42:1-4; 49:1-5; 50:4-11; 52:13–53:12) we come face to face with a Servant who will 'not faint or be discouraged till he has established justice in the earth' (42:4). God's chosen Servant (42:1) will faithfully and unwearyingly fulfil his calling. Nothing and no one will deflect or distract him from fulfilling the mission entrusted to his care. Not even personal despondency will turn him aside (49:4).

It is not surprising then that when the New Testament focuses on the cross it always does so from the perspective of Jesus' obedience. Explicitly or implicitly, the New Testament writers consistently highlight Jesus' obedience to the will of his Father. He had come from heaven, he said, not to do his own will, but the will of his heavenly Father (John 6:38). In his letter to the church in Rome, the apostle Paul described the whole course of Jesus' life as one seamless act of obedience: 'For as by the one man's [Adam's] disobedience the many were made sinners, so by the one man's [Jesus'] obedience the many will be made righteous' (Rom. 5:19). The cross was no unforeseen event; it was where Jesus had been destined to go in the will and purpose of God from times eternal. The whole course of our Lord's life from his conception in the Virgin Mary's womb until his ascension into heaven, was a life of undeviating obedience to the will of his Father. He was the obedient servant Adam failed to be. He was the servant who was 'obedient to the point of death, even death on a cross' (Phil. 2:8). Even when faced with the unimaginable suffering of the cross, he still prayed, 'not my will, but yours, be done' (Luke 22:42).

This life of servant obedience to his Father is the life that Jesus took to the cross. He was no dumb, uncomprehending sacrificial lamb. He was God's appointed and willing Lamb who had come to take away the sins of the world (John 1:29).

The Covenant Head

Romans 5:12-19 is one of the pivotal passages in the New Testament. There Paul explains how the sacrifice of Jesus on the cross effected the salvation of countless multitudes throughout history, both prior to Jesus' coming and after his ascension to God's right hand. In these verses, Paul compares and contrasts two men, Adam and Christ. Through one man, Adam, 'sin came into the world' (5:12). That 'one man's sin … brought condemnation' (5:12, 18) and 'many died through one man's trespass … and death reigned through that one man' (5:15, 17). In contrast, the other man, Jesus Christ, by his 'one act of righteousness' brought 'justification and life for all men' (5:18). Paul sums up the dramatic contrast in 5:19, 'For as by the one man's disobedience the many were made sinners, so by the one man's obedience the many will be made righteous.'

Paul is highlighting the intimate, inextricable relationship between Adam and those influenced by him, and Christ and those influenced by him. The relationship is one of representative headship. What one did affected everyone he represented. In modern democracies we are well acquainted with representative headship. Our government makes a decision and that decision holds for everyone under its jurisdiction.

You might be thinking, 'But is that fair? Is it fair that I should be affected by one man's sin millennia ago?' At least two responses can be made.

First, God is perfectly wise and perfectly good. All he does reflects who he is. He cannot act contrary to his nature. So, if God decrees it, we must conclude, whether we can understand it or not, that it is good and wise and right. This should be sufficient for Christians. Here and now we see through a glass darkly (1 Cor. 13:12), but one day we will see 'face to face' and all the shadows will disappear.

Second, just as we are affected by Adam's one sin because of our federal, covenant union with him, so we are affected by Christ's one act of obedience by virtue of our federal, covenant union with him. Justification, and salvation in all its parts, come to us because our God-appointed representative head secured them for us. The same representative or covenant headship that involved us in Adam's sin and brought us condemnation and death, brings us life and righteousness through Christ.

Jesus went to the cross unjustly condemned by Jewish and Roman authorities. But at the same time he went to the cross justly, bearing the righteous condemnation and judgment of God on our sin, in our place, as our covenant, representative head. The cross was not ultimately the expression of the wickedness of evil-hearted men, it was ultimately 'to show God's righteousness at the present time, so that he might be just and the justifier of the one who has faith in Jesus' (Rom. 3:26). As our covenant head, the Lord Jesus Christ justly bore God's wrath and condemnation upon our sin.

Before we move on one thing needs to be asserted. In himself, Jesus our covenant head was 'holy, innocent, unstained, separated from sinners' (Heb. 7:26). In him there was no sin. Only as a sinless covenant head could Jesus effectively represent sinners, live for them and die as a sin-atoning sacrifice for them. Only an unblemished lamb could be offered to God as a sin-atoning sacrifice. It is striking in Luke's account of Jesus' arraignment and trial (Luke 23), that on five separate occasions he highlights Jesus' personal innocence from all charges (verses 4, 14, 22, 41, 47). At the very moment of his earthly nadir, Jesus' personal innocence is attested from the mouths of the Roman governor, Pilate, from a justly condemned, but soon to be saved, criminal, and from a Roman centurion. In the pristine, perfect innocence of his holy humanity, Jesus died 'the righteous for the unrighteous, that he might bring us to God' (1 Pet. 3;18).

The Son of God's Love

The cross of Jesus Christ is the centrepiece of the Christian faith. Jesus was self-consciously aware that he had come into the world to die a sin-atoning death. At a significant turning point in his ministry, Jesus told his disciples that he had come not to be served but to serve and to give his life 'a ransom for many' (Mark 10:45). On the eve of his crucifixion he gathered his disciples to an upper room to eat the Passover with them (Mark 14:14). As they were eating, Jesus 'took bread, and after blessing it broke it and gave it to them, and said, "Take; this is my body." And he took a cup, and when he had given thanks he gave it to them, and they all drank of it. And he said to them, "This is my blood of the covenant, which is poured out for many"' (Mark 14:22-24; John 12:27; Gal. 6:14; 1 Cor. 1:18, 22-24).

But if we are to make any sense of the great transaction of Calvary, there is one thing we need to understand: the cross is the pulpit of God's love (Augustine). When the New Testament speaks of the cross, it always tells us that it was the provision of the Father's love (John 3:16; 1 John 4:9, 10; 2 Cor. 13:14; Rom. 5:5). In these, and other texts, it is the Father's love that is highlighted. Before it is anything else, the cross is the revelation of God's love. It is no less the revelation of his justice/righteousness, as we have seen (Rom. 3:25, 26). The cross was where God justly and righteously punished sin in the person of his own Son. But even this is imbedded in God's prior love.

If he had not been pleased to set his love upon us, there would have been no cross, no atonement for sin, no sin-bearing sacrifice! If we were to ask the question, 'Why did God make him who had no sin to be sin for us? (2 Cor. 5:21), the answer at the bottom of all other answers is, *Love*. The best known, and perhaps most loved verse in the Bible, puts it memorably: 'For God so loved the world, that he gave his only begotten Son' (John 3:16).

Undeserved, gracious, sovereign love is the fountain-head of the gospel. By nature we are 'children of [God's] wrath,' but God was pleased to set his special, saving love upon us in Christ. It is little wonder that every Christian heart regularly exclaims, 'Why, O Lord, such love to me?'[1]

John Owen, the seventeenth century English Puritan pastor understood this better than most. He exhorted his congregation and readers, 'Eye the Father as love; look not on him as an always lowering [forbidding] father, but as one most kind and tender. Let us look on him by faith, as one that hath had thoughts of kindness towards us from everlasting.'[2] So, Owen tells us that Christians must, therefore meditate on this distinguishing, free, unchangeable love. Because Owen never ceased to think and feel as a pastor, he anticipates a query from a dispir-ited, downcast believer: 'I cannot find my heart making returns of love unto God. Could I find my soul set upon

[1] From the hymn 'Sovereign Grace o'er Sin Abounding' by John Kent.

[2] John Owen, *Works*, vol. 2 (London: Banner of Truth Trust, 1966), p. 32.

him, I could then believe that his soul delighted in me.'
To this Owen responds,

> This is the most preposterous course that possibly thy
> thoughts can pitch upon … 'Herein is love,' saith the
> Holy Ghost, 'not that we loved God, but that he loved
> us' first, 1 John 4:10, 11. Now thou wouldst invert this
> order, and say, 'herein is love, not that God loved me,
> but that I loved him first' … This is a course of flesh's
> finding out that will never bring glory to God, nor
> peace to thy own soul. Lay down then, thy reasonings;
> take up the love of the Father upon a pure act of believ-
> ing, and that will open thy soul to let it out unto the
> Lord in the communion of love.[1]

The cross is the pulpit of God's love. The cross
proclaims to all, 'God so loved the world.' The great truth
here is not the *numbers* in the world, but the *badness* of
the world, 'God so loved the world.' This world that 'lies
in the power of the evil one' (1 John 5:19), the world that
lives in active, wilful rebellion against its Creator, the
world that is worthy of God's wrath is, astonishingly, the
recipient of his saving love.

---

[1] Owen, *Works*, vol. 2, p. 37.

CHAPTER II

'OH, THE DEPTH!'

I T is possible that we are to see an unfolding pattern
in Jesus' seven sayings. There may or may not be
significance in the number 'seven,' but a careful
examination of the chronological sequence of the seven
words reveals a thoughtful progression.

We see this, for example, in Jesus' first saying, 'Father
forgive them, for they know not what they do' (Luke
23:34). This remarkable saying is immediately followed
by his words to the dying thief, 'Truly I say to you, today
you will be with me in Paradise' (Luke 23:43). Here we
see our Lord living out the prayer he has just uttered to
his Father. As we reflect on the chronologically sequential
'cross words' of Jesus, we can recognize a theological and
spiritual progression. His words from the cross are not
random utterances. They are deeply related, revealing a
theology of the cross that marvellously displays the character of God.

So in Jesus' sayings from the cross the Lord is giving us a theology of the cross shaped and informed by his own words. Too often in the history of the church, systematic theology has been unmoored from its natural harbour, the historical, redemptive unfolding of God's saving grace revealed in the Scriptures. Theology has often been more shaped by the constraints, even demands, of logic, than God's supra-rational revelation in Holy Scripture. Herman Bavinck's conviction that 'Mystery is the life-blood of dogmatics,' has not always found its way into the theological systematizing of even conservative and evangelical scholars. This failure is best corrected when systematic theology is shaped and styled by the careful exegesis of God's word. Theology that is not exegetical of Holy Scripture cannot be truly Christian theology. Where theology is cohered and organized by the fruits of exegesis, it will inevitably bear the mark of 'mystery.' It will ever be ready to acknowledge that, to quote Bavinck again, the incomprehensibility of God is the fundamental thought in Christian dogmatics.

This conviction must be paramount in our thinking as we reflect on the cross of Christ. It is Jesus Christ, the eternal Word (John 1:1) who became flesh (John 1:14), who is expiring on the cross. But how can God die? Or, is it simply the humanity of Christ that is expiring on the cross? If so, how are we to think about the hypostatic union, the union in the one person of the God-Man of two natures? Or, does the cross show us God suffering?

But how can God suffer? God is surely not subject to outside forces, is he? Questions abound—good not inappropriate questions.

If God's word did not impress on us the out-of-this-world profundity of God and his ways, we would be at a loss to make any sense of the cross. But when we grasp that God and his ways are beyond our capacity to comprehend (Isa. 55:8, 9), we can rest with Paul in the happy contentment of humble adoration, exclaiming, 'Oh, the depth of the riches and wisdom and knowledge of God! How unsearchable are his judgments and how inscrutable his ways!' (Rom. 11:33).

There is a phrase in Hugh Martin's *The Shadow of Calvary* that highlights the unimaginable depths we are about to enter: 'the unfathomable abysses of the anguish of the Son of God.' The cross of Christ stands at the epicentre of the Christian faith and of every Christian's faith. The cross is to be the Christian's glory and supreme boast (Gal. 6:14). But there lies our greatest danger. Only too easily the glory of the cross, the glory of our sin-bearing, sin-atoning Saviour, can become a commonplace. Too much familiarity can breed casualness if not actual contempt. The remedy is not that we think, speak, and sing less about the cross. Rather we need the Holy Spirit to lead us day by day ever more deeply into 'the unfathomable abysses of the anguish of the Son of God.' Our Saviour is now risen and ascended. He is the Lamb in the midst of the throne (Rev. 7:17). But we must never forget what it cost God in Christ to rescue us from the guilt, condemnation, and power of our sin and reconcile us to himself. There is never a point in our Christian experience or understanding when we graduate beyond the cross. To the ages of eternity, God's ransomed and redeemed children will be plumbing the depths and scaling the heights of 'love divine.'

We are now in a position to reflect on the Lord Jesus Christ's dying words. He hangs on his cross, not as a wicked malefactor, but as an obedient, dearly loved Son, as a covenant Head, as God's sinless Lamb. He is where he is, not ultimately because wicked men have conspired against him and triumphed over him. He hangs on Calvary's cross 'according to the definite plan and foreknowledge of God' (Acts 2:23). Let us take to heart his dying words.

CHAPTER 12

JESUS' FIRST WORD FROM THE CROSS

Luke 23:34

THE first word from the cross is found in Luke 23:34, 'Father, forgive them, for they know not what they do.'

Try and take in the drama. Jesus has been arrested, scourged, forsaken by his own disciples, denied by Peter. But most astonishingly of all, this obedient and faithful Son, whom the Father delighted publicly to acknowledge and praise (Luke 3:22; 9:35), is being crucified 'according to the definite plan and foreknowledge of God' (Acts 2:23). As he hangs alone and forsaken by heaven and earth, Jesus is entering into the 'far country,' the abyss that our sin deserved. And he is where he is not merely as a man unjustly and inhumanely treated by the Jewish religious leaders. Jesus has been delivered up by his own

Father (Rom. 8:32), as the covenant head of his chosen people. He is not hanging on the cross as a private man; he is the divinely appointed Lamb of God who had come to die, the righteous in the place of the unrighteous (1 Pet. 3:18). On the cross Jesus is acting as a suffering Substitute. All that the old covenant sacrifices typified have come to their designed and decreed fulfilment in the offering up unto death of God's own Son in our flesh. The hymn writer captures the heart of this gracious and glorious provision from God for judgment-deserving sinners:

> Bearing shame and scoffing rude,
> In my place condemned He stood,
> Sealed my pardon with His blood,
> Hallelujah, what a Saviour![1]

But it would be only too easy to so focus on the divine drama of the cross that we downplay the physical sufferings of the Saviour. Jesus' whole body must have been wracked by excruciating pain. Crucifixion is unimaginably, excruciatingly painful. Every nerve-ending must have been crying out, 'No more, no more.' But Jesus is God's obedient Servant (Isa. 42:1-4), the better than Adam, who had resolved be 'obedient to the point of death, even death on a cross' (Isa. 42:3, 4; Phil. 2:8; John 6:38; Heb. 10:5-7).

It is as his body and mind are being torn asunder, that Jesus prays, 'Father, forgive them, for they know not what

---

[1] From the hymn 'Man of Sorrows, What a Name!' by Philip P. Bliss.

they do.' This is not a prayer uttered in quiet seclusion and contemplation. It is a prayer gasped by an expiring man, yet upheld by the Holy Spirit (Heb. 9:14). 'By this expression,' wrote John Calvin, 'Christ gave evidence that he was that mild and gentle lamb, which was to be led out to be sacrificed, as Isaiah the prophet had foretold, (Isa. 53:7).'[1]

Some time ago I read an article which said that the great truth shining out from Jesus' prayer is our need of God's forgiveness. It can hardly be doubted that Jesus is highlighting our great need of God's forgiveness. We all greatly need God's forgiveness, and Jesus' remarkable words confront us all with that great need. But the greater truth shining out from Jesus' words is not our need of forgiveness but the truth of God being a richly forgiving God. The first word from the cross was a word of mercy from a forgiving God. The cross is the supreme revelation of God, and it is a revelation of unimaginable love and mercy.

When Moses pleaded with the Lord to show him his glory, 'The Lord passed before him and proclaimed, "The Lord, the Lord, a God merciful and gracious, slow to anger and abounding in steadfast love and faithfulness"' (Exod. 34:6). This was not all the Lord said to Moses, but it was the first thing he said. This same note of divine grace and mercy is sounded throughout the New

---

[1] John Calvin, *Commentary on a Harmony of the Evangelists* (Grand Rapids: Baker, 1993), vol. xvii, p. 300.

Testament. In John 3:17 (words perhaps spoken by Jesus himself), we read, 'For God did not send his Son into the world to condemn the world, but in order that the world might be saved though him.'

This must be the first note that is struck in gospel preaching and witnessing. We must go on to spell out the dark background to God's love in Christ and the pressing need we all have to repent and turn to God for mercy. But the first movement of the gospel is to sound God's amazing, wholly gracious and completely undeserved love for judgment-deserving sinners.

These men, for whom Jesus is praying to his Father, have just crucified the Son of God, the Lord of glory. But the crucified Son of God prays for their salvation and restoration to God. This is what the Bible means by 'grace.' God's grace has often been described as 'undeserved kindness to judgment-deserving sinners.' This is true. But there is a danger that all too often 'grace' can be dislocated from its natural environment. Grace is not a special spiritual substance that God pours out on us. Grace is God personally acting in unimaginable kindness and saving mercy to men and women who deserve his just wrath. Grace is God giving us himself in his Son, the one who is 'full of grace and truth' (John 1:14). The *grace of God* is really the *God of grace*. Grace is personal and relational. It is not a 'blessing' taken by God from a heavenly treasury of merits and dispensed to undeserving sinners (that is a distinctly Roman Catholic understanding of grace). Grace is God in Christ giving us himself to be our Saviour, Lord, Helper, Restorer, Sanctifier, and never-failing Friend.

Love, Vast as the Ocean

Jesus' prayer tells us that, as yet, he had not lost his sense of being the Father's Son. In praying '*Father*,' the Lord's descent into the darkness of absolute abandonment, where there is no light, had not yet reached its deepest point. The darkness was increasing by the moment. The unimaginable forsakenness (Matt. 27:46) was at hand. But what occupies Jesus' thoughts is not his descent into the darkness, but the salvation of the men who had crucified him. He had told his disciples to love their enemies and to pray for those who persecuted them (Matt. 5:44). In doing so, they would show they truly were 'sons of your Father who is in heaven' (Matt. 5:45). Before the watching eyes of his disciples, and before their listening ears, Jesus practised what he preached. In doing so, he showed that he truly was the Son of his Father in heaven.

Any true theology of the cross will be dominated by the grace of God. I don't simply mean that the word 'grace' will be everywhere; rather, the God of grace will be everywhere.

Ignorantly and in Unbelief

To his prayer, Jesus appends a reason, 'for they do not know what they do.' These men who have just crucified

Jesus have no idea who he is and therefore no idea of the scale of the evil in which they are involved. They probably had not witnessed his miracles and heard none of his preaching. They acted ignorantly and in unbelief. There is a huge difference between sinning ignorantly and in unbelief, and sinning in the full face of the light, as the Pharisees did. This seems to be what Paul is saying in 1 Tim. 1:13. He received mercy, he tells us, 'because [he] acted ignorantly in unbelief.' Sin is sin and it is always culpable. But not all sin is equally culpable. Jesus spoke about the sin against the Holy Spirit, sin that saw the great works of God and heard the truth from the mouth of God in Christ, but which adamantly set itself against the light (Matt. 12:31). The writer to the Hebrews spoke about the impossibility of renewing to repentance men and women who experienced in some measure the power of God's truth in Christ but who crucified 'once again the Son of God to their own harm … holding him up to contempt' (Heb. 6:4-6; 10:26). Jesus is praying for men who had not yet reached the point of no return.

The Old Testament helps us to understand, in some measure, Jesus' prayer. In the Old Testament sacrificial rituals, blood was shed to symbolize the need for God to deal justly with sin and to wash us clean in order to fit us for his fellowship. But there was a sin for which no sacrifice was offered. 'Unintentional' sins and sins of omission were dealt with in the sin offering. These were sins people committed in ignorance of the Mosaic code or when they forgot those laws they had learned. Sins committed with a 'high hand' were not covered (Num. 15:22-31). A high-handed sin is one a professing believer commits boldly and defiantly, not caring about the consequences and feeling no guilt about it once committed. It is a sin people commit fearlessly as they shake their fists, literally or figuratively, at the Lord. A sin committed with a high hand is not always the same thing as an intentional sin. All high-handed sins are intentional but not all intentional sins are high-handed. The sin against the Holy Spirit is defiant unbelief in the face of God's love and grace in Christ. It is sinning against the light. This is the context of Jesus' deeply solemn words in Mark 3:28:30: '"Truly, I say to you, all sins will be forgiven the children of man, and whatever blasphemies they utter, but whoever blasphemes against the Holy Spirit never has forgiveness, but is guilty of an eternal sin"— for they were saying, "He has an unclean spirit."'

It is deeply solemn to think that there is such a thing as 'a point of no return,' a point beyond which God confirms us in our chosen unbelief and leaves us to reap its unspeakable consequences. No one knows when that point of no return is reached. So it is vital, as the writer to the Hebrews reminds us, to 'go on to maturity … 'looking to Jesus, the founder and perfected of our faith' (Heb. 6:1; 12:2).

Sin has a way of increasingly hardening our hearts and shutting our minds to the truth of the gospel. Slowly, but surely, the soul-deadening influence of sin can creep over our souls and confirm us in resolute unbelief. There is the awful possibility that 'if we go on sinning deliberately after receiving the knowledge of the truth, there no longer remains a sacrifice for sins, but a fearful expectation of judgment and a fury of fire that will consume the adversaries' (Heb. 10:26). It is little wonder that Paul could write, 'Behold, now is the favourable time; behold now is the day of salvation' (2 Cor. 6:2)

Jesus' High Priestly Intercession

In uttering this first cry from the cross, our Lord entered that work of intercession which he ever lives to continue on our behalf (Heb. 7:25). He thinks, not of himself, but of others; he is occupied not with his own pain but with their sins. He makes no threat but instead offers a tender prayer of pleading intercession.

When was that prayer answered? Later in Luke 23, The evangelist tells us of the effect Jesus' dying and death had on the centurion in charge of the death squad. This man, says Luke, praised God saying, 'Certainly this man was innocent' (Luke 23:47). Was the centurion the firstfruit of Jesus' high priestly, merciful intercession? Seven weeks after this, on the day of Pentecost, three thousand of these people, whom Peter described as the murderers of Christ, repented and believed; and, in the days that followed, thousands more, including 'a great many of the priests' (Acts 2:47; 4:4; 6:7). That was the remarkable answer to Jesus' prayer and it has continued down the centuries.

Every sinner who turns to God for mercy in the name of Jesus Christ will certainly receive mercy. Such saved sinners are the fruit of Jesus' prayer, 'Father, forgive them.'

So the first word from the cross is a word pleading for pardon for sinners. God's forgiveness is still today the greatest need of every person in our world. We all have many needs, some of them perhaps very pressing and urgent. But towering above all our needs is our need of God's mercy. The wonderful thing is that what we most desperately need, God delights to give. The God of the Bible takes no pleasure in the death of the wicked. More than that, the God of the Bible personally pleads with men and women to turn to him and live (Ezek. 33:11).

One of the most remarkable statements in the Bible is found in 2 Corinthians 5:20. There Paul writes, 'we are ambassadors for Christ, God making his appeal through us. We implore you on behalf of Christ, be reconciled to God.' Have you responded to God's imploring appeal and put your trust alone in God's own Son who died, the righteous for the unrighteous, to bring us to God?

Practising the Gospel

If we were to leave things there, we would be doing a severe injustice to the salvation Jesus died and rose again to secure for us. For in the New Testament there is an inner dynamic, even logic, to the saving work of Christ that transforms how Christians live.

First, in his letter to the Ephesians, Paul uses a compelling logic to persuade the believers in Ephesus to practise the grace of forgiveness:

> Be kind to one another, tender hearted, forgiving one another, as God in Christ forgave you. Therefore be imitators of God, as beloved children (Eph. 4:31–5:1).

How can we say we have received God's forgiveness and not fully and freely forgive those who have sinned against us? Jesus said, 'Freely you have received, freely give.' An unforgiving heart is a sign of an unforgiven heart.

Second, in Psalm 130:4, the Psalmist says to God, 'with you there is forgiveness, that you may be feared.' Not only is the reception into our hearts and lives of God's gracious forgiveness in Christ to change how we treat one another, it is also to change how we relate to God himself. The cost to God of forgiving sinners in the sacrifice of his own Son, is, surely, to humble us and cause us to stand in awe and wonder before the God who spared not his only Son but gave him up for us all (Rom. 8:32).

Jesus' first words from the cross highlight the grace of the gospel, or better the grace of Christ who is the gospel. Every Christian, every Christian church, and perhaps especially every Christian preacher is to be noted by both the proclamation and the practice of the grace of God in Christ. Nothing more beautifies a Christian's profession of faith than a lifestyle of grace, treating other people as God in Christ has treated us.

CHAPTER 13

JESUS' SECOND WORD FROM THE CROSS

Luke 23:43

I T has been said that crucifixion is the most painful way to die. The physical pain and emotional turmoil must have consumed Jesus as he hung on the cross. And yet, with the little strength he had (for Jesus' humanity was a true humanity) Jesus spoke words that shall forever be remembered from the cross. The words must have been audible but they were surely excruciating for the Saviour to speak them. Once again we see the selflessness of Jesus. The pressing needs of others always took precedence over his own needs. Instead of being consumed with his own degradation and humiliation, Jesus is alert to the need of a soon-to-die sinner who begs him for mercy.

We know that at first this man and the other thief were both hostile to Jesus (Mark 15:32). But now he is asking Jesus, pleading with Jesus, to remember him when he comes into his kingdom. What has happened to this man? What brought about the transformation in his attitude to Jesus? Clearly the Holy Spirit had been at work in his life, out of sight of those who were watching the degrading spectacle. No one ever again came to faith as this dying thief did, he was quite unique in his conversion.

Here was a faith that was able (better, *enabled*) to see the glory of Jesus at its most hidden. Jesus is hanging, stripped not only of divine majesty but of all human dignity. He is hanging helpless, battered, bloodied, derided. The cross had blown away the faith of Jesus' own disciples and killed their hopes (Luke 24:21). But this man, at the lowest point of Jesus' self-emptying, when his messianic identity was most obscured, proclaims him a king and prays, 'Jesus, remember me when you come into your kingdom.' Is this not astounding? Calvin comments:

> Consider his plight. He is close to death, and suffers awful torment as he waits for someone to come and break his legs and dismember him—torture so bitter and terrifying as to make him lose both mind and memory. He sees our Lord Jesus Christ hanging there, like him, and suffering the greater disgrace. Yet what does he say? He not only acknowledges his faults humbly before God, not only assumes the role of teacher so as to bring his companion back to the right path, but makes a confession which, when we look at the facts closely, deserves to surpass all others.[1]

[1] Quoted by Robert White in John Calvin, *Crucified and Risen* (Edinburgh: Banner of Truth Trust, 2020), p. xiv.

In response Jesus says to him, 'I tell you the truth, today you will be with me in paradise.' The conversion of the dying thief was surely one of the most remarkable conversions recorded for us in the Bible. The Bible is relatively uninterested in how men and women are brought to saving faith in Jesus. It is deeply concerned that men and women, however they come, do come to Christ. There are a number of features that call out for consideration.

First, what was it that converted the criminal? There is no doubt that every conversion is the sovereign work of God. In the new birth, God is absolutely sovereign and must be so (John 3:3-8). But ordinarily God uses 'means' to bring about his saving purposes. What, humanly speaking, caused the transformation in this dying thief? One moment he was openly reviling Jesus and the next, or so it seemed, he was pleading for mercy. Was it Jesus' first word from the cross, 'Father forgive them'? Was it what Jesus did not say? The Saviour is hanging reviled and bloodied and forsaken, but he does not revile in return (1 Pet. 2:23). Was this near-expiring man convicted by the Saviour's humble, cross-embracing demeanour? We are not told, perhaps deliberately.

The fewest words can be used by the Holy Spirit to work wonders. When Jesus evangelized the Samaritan woman, her brief testimony, 'Come see a man who told me all that I ever did,' had a profound gospel impact on her village (John 4:25-38). In the new birth, the Holy

Spirit, like the wind, 'blows where he wills' (John 3:6-8). John the Baptist was regenerated in his mother's womb (Luke 1:32). God uses means or no means as it pleases him.

But surely we can say more. Was it not the out-of-this-world demeanour of Jesus that pierced this man's heart? Peter encouraged Christian wives to live such godly lives that their husbands might be won to Christ 'without a word' (1 Pet. 3:1-8). We vastly under-estimate the power and attractiveness of a godly life. The impact of a humble, holy, providence-embracing life can 'speak' volumes. There is surely little doubt that this dying thief was powerfully impacted by the dying grace of Jesus.

In the early church evangelism was not an activity of the church; it was the church's daily lifestyle. J. I. Packer described evangelism as 'a Christian living as a Christian in the world.' This is not to say that organized evangelism is out of place. Indeed, our Lord Jesus Christ commanded his church to go to all the ethnic or language groups in the world and 'make disciples of all nations, baptizing them in the name of the Father and of the Son and of the Holy Spirit, teaching them to observe all that I have commanded you. And behold, I am with you always, to the end of the age' (Matt. 28:19, 20). The church of Jesus Christ is a missionary oriented church. But the witness of the early church, and what powerfully impacted the pagan world of the day, was the transformed, counter-cultural lives of believers. Jesus truly was Lord. They lived for him and were willing to die for him. The gospel had transformed their lives, spiritually, morally, socially. Until the Saviour's words, 'By this will all men know that you are my disciples, that you love one another' (John 13:34, 35), capture the hearts and minds of professing Christians, our gospel witness will be devoid of power and grace.

There is much talk today about 'revitalizing the church.' The church truly needs revitalizing. The question is, How will this happen? The New Testament Gospels and letters were written to Christians living under the authoritarian rule of Rome. The religion of Rome was syncretistic, idols of all kinds abounded. The penalties for being a Christian could be severe, even deadly. Into that darkly pagan, Christ-denying world, God's people were instructed and nurtured by the twin gifts of the Holy Spirit and the Holy Scriptures. What is remarkable as you read through the four Gospels, Paul's letters and the other New Testament Scriptures, is the complete absence of teaching on 'how to evangelize.' The great concern is not how to reach into and engage with neighbours and society in general. What is emphasized is the vital importance of living such godly, Christlike lives that opportunities for witness will inevitably arise. Christian wives are told, 'be subject to your own husbands, so that even if some do not obey the word, they may be won without a word by the conduct of their wives, when they see your respectful and pure conduct' (1 Pet. 3:1, 2). Christians in general are told, 'in your hearts honour Christ the Lord as holy, always being prepared to make a defence to anyone who asks you for a reason for the hope that is in you; yet do it with gentleness and respect, having a good conscience, so that, when you are slandered, those who revile your good behaviour in Christ may be put to shame' (1 Pet. 3:15, 16). Jesus himself impressed this truth on his disciples: 'You are the light of the world. A city set on a hill cannot be hidden. Nor do people light a lamp and put it under a basket, but on a stand, and it gives light to all in the house. In the same way, let your light shine before others, so that they may see your good works and give glory to your Father who is in heaven' (Matt. 5:14-16).

Second, we should note that Jesus has not yet reached the point of forsakenness. As he spoke these words to the dying thief, he was yet relatively calm and collected. Jesus' experience on the cross was a moment by moment escalation of suffering. He has yet to enter into the omega point of forsakenness. So in the midst of his suffering, Jesus is enabled to minister the grace of God to a dying man. For this one man Jesus' death on the cross literally brought him life.

Your extremity might well be the means God uses to bring someone savingly to himself! When God brings his children into 'deep waters,' he promises to be with them. More than that, he promises that all things will work together for the good of those who love him, those whom he has called into his kingdom and fellowship (Rom. 8:28). In his unimaginable extremity, the Lord

Jesus Christ ministered saving grace to a dying man. With God, you just never know.

Third, Jesus' words shed light on where he was between his death and resurrection. He said to the dying thief, 'Truly, I say to you, today you will be with me in Paradise.' 'Paradise' is mentioned also in 2 Corinthians 12:4 and Revelation 2:7. Paradise is the presence of God. While his body lay in the tomb, Jesus' human soul was rejoicing in the presence of his Father, acclaimed by angels, adored by the redeemed. This is the 'Paradise' the dying thief would soon be enjoying.

But the Christian hope is not the immortality of the soul; it is the resurrection of the body (1 Cor. 15:12-58). The reunion of Jesus' soul with his body on the third day is a template and harbinger of what awaits every Christian. This unnatural separation of soul and body is the reason why Christians 'groan inwardly' (Rom. 8:23). Our full and final salvation awaits 'the redemption of our bodies' (Rom. 8:23). One day the Lord Jesus 'will transform our lowly body to be like his glorious body, by the power that enables him even to subject all things to himself' (Phil. 3:21).

This leaves us asking the question, Where was Jesus' body when he was in Paradise immediately after his death? His body was in the tomb, watched over and kept by the power of the Holy Spirit from decay, until it was reunited with his glorified soul on the third day.

Fourth, we should notice the words 'with me.' The thief had asked Jesus to remember him when he came into his kingdom. What was Jesus' response? 'Today you will be with me in Paradise.' '*With me.*' He answered the man's dying prayer above and beyond all his asking. Even as he hung on the cross, Jesus knew that being with him was the glory of heaven.

There is a self-conscious egocentricity in Jesus' words. But it is the egocentricity of truth. All through the Gospels Jesus preached *himself.* He said, 'Come to *me*, all who labour and are heavy laden, and I will give you rest' (Matt. 11:28). John's Gospel is punctuated with Jesus' self-conscious egocentricity: '*I* am the bread of life'; '*I* am the light of the world'; '*I* am the door'; '*I* am the Good Shepherd'; '*I* am the resurrection and the life'; '*I* am the way, the truth and the life'; '*I* am the true vine'. '*I* am … *I* am … *I* am …' The Lamb truly is all the glory in Immanuel's land!

Fifth, the dying thief understood that Jesus was a king with a kingdom, 'Remember me when you come into your kingdom.' Israel had been waiting for and hoping for God's long promised king. 'Somehow,' this dying thief had come to understand that Jesus was that king. As he looked on the crucified Jesus and heard his dying words, this man made the connection. Here, hanging bloodied and nailed to a Roman cross, was God's King. The man's confession was surely one of the most remarkable conversion testimonies the world has ever heard.

Saving faith sees beyond the seen to the unseen. What could this man see with his physical eyes? A humiliated, spit bespattered, deserted, nail-pierced fellow human being. But with the eye of faith he saw beyond and behind the veil—he saw God's King. Paul told the church in Ephesus that he prayed that God would enlighten the eyes of their hearts (Eph 1:17), so that they would know the rich blessings that were their gospel inheritance in Christ. Our hearts have 'eyes.' Paul, of course, is speaking about spiritual sight, the insight and understanding that the Holy Spirit graciously gives to us. So it was with this dying thief: he saw what no one else appeared to see; he saw a king on a cross.

Do you 'see'? Perhaps the very first evidence of the new birth is spiritual sight (John 3:3-8). When an infant is born into the world, they come out of nine months of virtual darkness into a world of light. So it is in the new birth. The Holy Spirit comes to open sin-blinded minds and hearts to the glorious, saving truth of God's love in Jesus Christ. This dying man could say as his breath expired, 'Once I was blind, but now I see.'

Finally, we cannot miss that the dying thief's conversion was remarkable and last minute. There was a uniqueness to this man's conversion. No one would ever again be converted the way he was. But can we doubt that he is set before us in the gospel to give hope to the most despairing.

We should never despair of the conversion of anyone, no matter how seemingly impossible it appears. Never despair; neither for yourself nor for anyone else. Everyone looking on would have thought that the dying thief was going to hell, but he was heading for heaven. He is a wonderful example of the sovereignty of God in salvation. God's sovereignty is never intended to leave us perplexed. It is always intended to humble us and encourage us. 'Is anything too hard for the Lord?'

CHAPTER 14

JESUS' THIRD WORD FROM THE CROSS

John 19:26, 27

J ESUS' words to his mother and to John his disciple are probably his third saying from the cross. There is nothing of the pulse quickening drama of the first two sayings. But what Jesus says is deeply revealing. The true character of faith is seen not when all is well with us, but when our life is engulfed in sore and crushing providences. Jesus is the perfect example of the man of faith. He is our pattern and the example we are to follow (1 Pet. 2:21-23). In the unimaginable extremity of his suffering on the cross, he lived out what it means to live by faith.

First, the theological significance of Jesus' words, 'Behold your son,' should be pondered. One of the marked features of John's Gospel is the use of 'double entendres.' One example would be John 3:3, 'unless a man is born again [or, 'born from above'] he cannot enter the kingdom of heaven.' When Jesus says to Mary, 'Woman, behold, your son' (John 19:26), it is possible that we are being encouraged to see a double meaning. Jesus is not simply commanding Mary *to look on John from this moment on* as her son, as God's kind provision for her care in her hour of deepest need; he is saying, 'Woman, behold your son,' that is, Mary is being commanded to behold, *to reflect seriously on the dying form of the fruit of her womb.* This expiring man is her son. Later Mary will understand that his sufferings were not for sins he had done; he is where he is as the God-provided substitute lamb of sacrifice for the sins of his people.

Second, in his words to Mary and to John, Jesus is exemplifying a commandment-obedient life. He had come into the world not to abolish God's law but to fulfil it (Matt. 5:17-20). One of the ways he fulfilled God's law was by perfectly keeping its every precept. In his thoughtful, tender care of his mother, Jesus is fulling the fifth commandment, 'Honour your father and mother' (Exod. 20:12).

Jesus had told his disciples, 'If you love me, keep my commandments.' Now he practises what he preaches. He loves his Father, so he obeys his Father's commandments. Jesus is the model Servant of the Lord. He lives to please his Father and what pleases his Father is a commandment-loving and commandment-obeying life. Are you pleasing the heavenly Father? Are God's commandments your 'happy choice'?

Keeping God's commandments when life is sweet is one thing; keeping them when all your circumstances are in opposition to God's promises is another. When all hell was let loose on Jesus, he exemplified not only filial love, but also and more fundamentally a heart fixed on keeping his Father's commandments.

Third, earlier in the Gospel narrative, Jesus had appeared to minimize the importance of family ties—see Mark 3:31-35 and Matthew 10:37. There are few more heart-searching words in the Bible. We need often to ask ourselves if the Lord truly has our primary allegiance and the first claim on our love and service.

But the Bible no less impresses on us the importance and significance of family. Giving the Lord our first and exclusive allegiance must never become an excuse for neglecting family. Using Christian service as an excuse for not giving quality time to our family and cherishing everyone in our family with generosity and kindness, is an affront to God and a denial of the gospel (1 Tim. 5:8).

Here in the midst of his sufferings, Jesus expresses the tenderest care and compassion for his mother. The pain must have been all but unendurable, but to the last Jesus is sensitive to the needs of others. As he hung on the cross, Jesus revealed the selfless concern of God. He had come into the world not to be served, but to serve and to give his life a ransom for the many (Mark 10:45). The needs of others always took precedence over his own. This truth lies at the heart of the cross. The Son of God, who was in everything equal with God, 'emptied himself, taking the form of a servant ... and became obedient unto death, even the death of a cross (Phil. 2:5-8).

Reading Jesus' words to Mary and to John, surely prompt us to ask, Why, when he is being offered up as the propitiation for the sins of the whole world (1 John 2:2), enduring unimaginable pain, and about to descend into the abyss of God forsakenness, was Jesus thinking about his mother? Did he not have 'bigger' things to think about? Clearly not. With the weight of the world's sin crushing the life out of his soul, Jesus cared for his mother. The remarkable intimacy and individuality of Jesus' love for needy men and women is beautifully highlighted. Just as the Saviour did not die for sin 'in the lump'[1] but for each individual sin, so his care is not for sinners 'in the lump' but for individual sinners.

These verses pose a huge question for all who profess to be Christians. How much of the self-denying mind of our Saviour is in us and among us? If the Lord has indeed come to dwell within us (John 14:23), should not something of his selfless life be reflected in how we treat one another?

Fourth, why did Jesus not entrust his mother to his brothers, Mary's own sons? Why to John? The simple answer is, as one commentator simply put it, John was there, his brothers were not! But there is another answer.

---

[1] *Works of Thomas Goodwin* (Edinburgh: James Nichol, 1863), 'Christ the Mediator,' vol. 5, p. 187.

The spiritual bonds of God's people run deeper than the natural bonds of family ties. Jesus is living out his own words (see Matt. 10:37!).

Fifth, we should notice that Jesus calls Mary 'Woman' and not 'mother'? Why does he do this? Calling Mary 'woman' seems at first blush to be somewhat offhand. He did the same thing in John 2 at the wedding in Cana. Why? To impress on Mary that her primary connection with him must first be one of faith not blood. Jesus is her son; but he is first her Lord (Mark 3:31-35).

Back to our Lord's words. What is so striking above all else is the sheer humanity and tenderness of Jesus' words. Think with me about the 'pictures of God' that confront us in the Bible. First, Isaiah 40:10, 11, an exquisite picture of strength and power combined with tenderness and gentleness. Isaiah 42:2-4, a beautiful picture of unyielding resolve and unwearyingly gentleness. Matthew 11:28-30, the most magnificent picture of the Lord of glory inviting—*tenderly* inviting—weary, worn and sad sinners to come to him.

This leaves me to ask: Do you sufficiently take to heart what our God reveals to us about himself in the Bible? Too many Christians think of him like the servant in the parable, 'I knew you to be a hard man' (Matt. 25:24); or like the older brother in the parable of the prodigal son, 'Look, these many years I have slaved for you' (Luke 15:29). Does that describe you? Jesus is the perfect revelation of God (John 1:18). There is no un-Christlikeness in

God. There is not another kind of God lurking behind our Lord Jesus Christ. The God-Man of Calvary is the God of eternity. In his thoughtful, kind, self-disregarding words to his mother, the Lord is saying, 'Behold your God.' In these words to his no doubt bewildered and grieving mother, Jesus was revealing what God is like in his care and compassion for his earthly mother.

This is what God-ness looks like and sounds like. Paul later wrote to the church in Ephesus, 'Be imitators of God as beloved children' (Eph. 5:1, 2; John 13:35). This is an epic challenge to Christians. It searches out our hearts. As Paul continues in Ephesians, we can see what being an imitator of God meant to him: It meant being 'kind to one another, tenderhearted, forgiving one another, as God in Christ forgave you (Eph. 4:32). It meant walking 'in love, as Christ loved us and gave himself up for us, a fragrant offering and sacrifice to God' (Eph. 5:1). It meant that 'sexual immorality and all impurity or covetousness must not even be named among you, as is proper among saints' (Eph. 5:3). Does this begin to describe you?

CHAPTER 15

JESUS' FOURTH WORD FROM THE CROSS

Matthew 27:46

Jesus' cry of forsakenness is among the most unfathomable statements in the Bible. We stand in amazed wonder as we read John 1:14, 'And the Word [God's eternal Word, his eternal Fellow, cf. John 1:1, 2] became flesh.' We stand perhaps in even more amazed wonder as we read Matthew 27:46, 'My God, my God, why have you forsaken me?' All through his earthly life, Jesus heard his Father punctuating history with the words, 'This is my beloved Son' (Matt. 3:17; 17:5). But now heaven is silent. Jesus is quoting the opening words of Psalm 22. It is as if he could find no human words of his own to express what his experience of being the sin-bearing Saviour meant. We will make no sense whatever of Jesus' cry—and it was a cry, a pain-filled, heart-rending cry—unless we understand who he is and why he is where he is.

Who is this man who cries, 'My God, my God, why have you forsaken me?' He is the eternal Son of God. He is the eternal Son of God made flesh, and made flesh for a specific purpose, to 'save his people for their sins' (Matt. 1:21). Jesus is where he is for one reason, he is representing sinners. He is not hanging alone and abandoned on a Roman cross because he was guilty of some dreadful crime. He is the covenant, representative head who has come to rescue us by substituting himself for us. It is our sins, not his own, that he is bearing on the cross. It is the forsakenness that our sins deserved that he is experiencing.

There are at least three things we need to note as we begin to consider this cry of all cries.

First, Jesus is on the cross in obedience to his Father. Jesus declared, 'I have come down from heaven, not to do my own will but the will of him who sent me' (John 6:38). There were opportunities for Jesus to avoid the cross, but he refused every one of them. We see Jesus' obedience to the will of his Father in his agony in the garden of Gethsemane. As the shadow of the cross began to penetrate his human soul, Jesus prayed, 'My Father, if it be possible, let this cup pass from me; nevertheless, not as I will but as you will' (Matt. 26:39; see also verses 42 and 44). No matter the pain, the humiliation, the mental and spiritual darkness, Jesus would do what Adam failed to do, he would be 'obedient unto death.'

Second, he is on the cross because of the heavenly Father's love for a world of lost sinners. Whenever the

New Testament speaks of the love of God it almost always is thinking of the love of the Father: 'For God so loved the world, that he gave his only Son' (John 3:16). 'In this is love, not that we loved God but that he loved us and sent his Son to be the propitiation for our sins' (1 John 4:10). The texts could be multiplied. Octavius Winslow, as we have noted, memorably captured this truth: 'Who delivered up Jesus to die? Not the Jews for envy. Not Pilate for fear. Not Judas for money. *But the Father for love.*'

Third, Jesus is there because of his love for his sheep. We are never to think that the love of the Father was not perfectly mirrored in his own Son. Paul could write, 'the Son of God … loved me and gave himself for me' (Gal. 2:20).

The fundamental question we need to consider is, What did it mean for Jesus to be 'forsaken' by his Father?

We first need to say what it did not mean. It did not mean there was a rupture in the Holy Trinity. God is eternally One in his Threeness and Three in his Oneness.

Nor did it mean that Jesus only 'felt' he was forsaken. He does not ask why he 'feels' forsaken, but why he 'is' forsaken. The Son of God united to our flesh was forsaken, truly and really, by his Father. The agony and drama of the cross is not an illusion, a charade. So, what did it mean for Jesus to be forsaken?

If ever we are on holy ground it is here. There are depths we cannot begin to plumb. As the incarnate Son of God hung on Calvary's cross, it may be best if we put our hands to our mouths and say, 'It is the Lord.' Here we are out of our depth. But while we are assuredly out of our depth, we must not remain silent.

First, Jesus' cry was, of necessity, a cry of sinless perfection. Only as the sinless Lamb of God could Jesus make effective atonement for sin. But it is precisely in his sinlessness that we begin, if only marginally, to understand the anguish of his cry, 'My God, my God, why have you forsaken me?' All the lights have gone out for Jesus. What bewilders him is the absence of the sense of the presence of his Father. God loves holiness and he especially delights in perfect holiness. And yet here is Jesus, the holy, spotless Son of God, and heaven is silent and darkness, the darkness of holy wrath is engulfing his soul. This for Jesus is the unfathomable conundrum; the God who is of purer eyes than to look on sin, has forsaken him the Sinless One. You might ask, But does he not know that he is the sin-bearing Substitute of his people? Yes and no. You must not think the humanity of our Saviour was all-knowing. If it had been, he could not be the Saviour we need. He would be a divinized man, a divine-human hybrid. But he 'became flesh,' taking to himself our limitedness and creatureliness. It is little wonder the Sinless One cried out and asked 'Why?'

Second, it was a cry of sin-bearing substitution. Jesus is experiencing the righteous judgment of God that our sins deserved. He is hanging on the cross as the God-provided

Substitute of his people. He is dying 'the righteous for the unrighteous' to bring us to God (1 Pet. 3:18). The awful and unimaginable penalty that our sin deserved was being poured out on God's sinless Son:

> Bearing shame and scoffing rude,
> In my place condemned he stood.[1]

Third, It was a cry of bruised but unbowed faith and trust. As the darkness engulfed his soul, as his mind was tortured beyond our imagining, as his whole being cried out in an unfathomable agony, he refused to let God go. Yes, the sense of God as '*Abba*' had gone. But the Saviour's faith, buffeted, bruised, and tormented, remained firm: '*My* God, *my* God.' Notice the personal pronoun. It was Martin Luther who said that the Christian faith rested on personal pronouns.

But the question still remains, What did all this mean for him?

It meant, *first*, that fellowship with his Father was lost. He has no longer any sense of the Father *as Father*. All he can say is, 'My God, my God, why have you forsaken me?' This is the only occasion, even on the cross, when Jesus does not call God his Father. He did so in the agony of Gethsemane. He also prayed, 'Father, forgive them.' But now all he can say is, 'My God, my God.' All sense of God as '*Abba*' has gone. Father and Son had gone up together to Calvary, and throughout his life he was never

---

[1] From the hymn 'Man of Sorrows, What a Name' by Philip P. Bliss.

alone; but now there is no sense of his divine Sonship and no sense of the Father's love. There is no voice from heaven to reassure him, only utter silence.

It is impossible for us to begin to plumb the 'immensities and infinities' of the Saviour's desolation. But here we must pause. It must never be thought that the fellowship the Son, as God the Son, enjoyed with his Father was lost even for one moment. While we must never underplay the cry of dereliction, we must never imagine that the cry signalled a fundamental break in the '*koinonia*' of the Holy Trinity. In becoming flesh (John 1:14), God's eternal Word, his only begotten Son, did not cease to be who he eternally was. Even as he sucked in Mary's milk to nourish and sustain his humanity, the Son of God was upholding the universe by his powerful word. And even as he cried out 'My God, my God why have you forsaken me?' he continued to uphold the universe he had created.

Here we are out of our depth. Our Saviour's humanity was a true humanity. His two natures were inseparable, but never confused, or mixed, or divided. This great mystery was the focus of the Fourth Ecumenical Church Council at Chalcedon in A.D. 451 Rather than attempt to unravel the unfathomable, the Council declared,

> We teach ... one and the same Christ, Son, Lord, Only-begotten, known in two natures, without confusion, without change, without division, without separation.

It should not surprise us that we are out of our depth. The apostle Paul affirmed, 'Great indeed, we confess, is the mystery of godliness: He was manifested in the flesh' (1 Tim. 3:16).

Second, it meant he was experiencing the weight of the divine wrath that our sin deserved. God was making him who had no sin to be sin for us (2 Cor. 5:21). What is hell? It is the absence of the gracious presence of God and the unending experience of his holy wrath. All support has been withdrawn from Jesus, the support of his Father's presence and love, and the support of the Father's common grace. There was no human support or consolation, only unrelieved aloneness. The Saviour of the world, the Lord of glory, is devoted to destruction.

But the question may be asked, Did he not know that he had a future? Had he forgotten the covenant of redemption? Had he forgotten that he would rise on the third day? Everything was eclipsed, only darkness reigned. The darkness that covered the face of the earth was symbolic of the darkness that covered his human soul.

What can we say about the Lord as he was experiencing the just wrath of his Father against our sin? We can say he was being upheld by the Holy Spirit in fulfilment of God's promise in Isaiah 42:1, 'Behold my servant, whom I uphold, my chosen, in whom my soul delights; I have put my Spirit upon him' (read Heb. 9:14). It is important we understand that the cross was the concerted, agreed work of the Holy Trinity. In his humanity, Jesus was upheld and enabled by the Holy Spirit to be obedient unto the death he committed himself to in the eternal covenant of redemption.

We can say, *thirdly*, that Jesus' forsakenness was real. If it were not real that would mean he did not experience as our covenant head the judgment of God that our sins deserved. His forsakenness was not imagined, it was real. Just as our sin is real, not imagined, so the penalty God decreed for our sin is real not imagined. Jesus truly entered into the forsakenness, the God-abandonment, that my sin deserved. But as the Father was forsaking him as he bore our sin and condemnation, he was surely also delighting in the Son whom he loved eternally, the Son who was 'obedient unto death, even the death of the cross.'

It is in Jesus' cry that we, more than anywhere else, are given to see the sinfulness of sin. What must sin be if it took the God-forsakenness of God's own Son to atone for it? How are we even to begin to measure the awfulness of sin? It is only really here that we come to have any sense of the sheer awfulness of sin. Our great problem is that we think of sin too horizontally—the mess it makes of ourselves and others (and this should not be ignored). But the real horror of sin is that it is rebellion against our Maker; it is a despising of his love, a defiance of his commandments, a repudiation of Jesus and his cross. King David was expressing not only his own sense of the sinfulness of sin, but the true heart of sin, when he wrote, 'Against you and you only have I sinned' (Psa. 51:4). When you are next tempted to sin, little or big, think on this: 'If I yield to this temptation, I am despising God's love, defiantly trampling on his commandments, and repudiating Jesus and his cross, mocking his forsakenness.'

Let me close this word from the cross with the words of Isaac Watts:

> Alas! and did my Saviour bleed,
>   And did my Sovereign die,
> Would He devote that sacred head
>   For such a worm as I?
>
> Was it for crimes that I had done
>   He groaned upon the tree?
> Amazing pity, grace unknown,
>   And love beyond degree!
>
> Well might the sun in darkness hide,
>   And shut its glories in,
> When God, the incarnate Maker, died
>   For man, His creature's sin.
>
> Thus might I hide my blushing face
>   While His dear cross appears;
> Dissolve my heart in thankfulness,
>   And melt mine eyes to tears.
>
> But drops of grief can ne'er repay
>   The debt of love I owe.
> Here, Lord, I give myself away!
>   'Tis all that I can do.

CHAPTER 16

JESUS' FIFTH WORD FROM THE CROSS

John 19:28

THE darkest moment of Jesus' experience on the cross had passed. Soon Jesus will say, 'It is finished' (John 19:30). But before that he says, 'I thirst.' Two little but deeply significant words. What do they say and signify? Here is the Maker of heaven and earth and he has parched lips. The Lord of glory is in need of a drink. The Bible never tries to airbrush the weaknesses or even the fears of the Lord Jesus Christ. There is no attempt to present an idealized and ultimately unreal Saviour.

We do well to remember as we read God's word, that every word is significant: 'All Scripture is breathed out by God and profitable for teaching, for reproof, for correction, and for training in righteousness, that the man of God may be competent, equipped for every good work'

(2 Tim. 3:16, 17). The words 'I thirst' are more than simply a touch of colour to heighten John's narrative. There is a rich theology embedded in these two little words.

We see here two reasons why Jesus said 'I thirst'.

1. All Was Now Finished

John Calvin comments thus:

> Now, it ought to be remarked, that Christ did not ask anything to drink till all things have been accomplished; and thus he testifies his infinite love towards us, and the inconceivable earnestness of his desire to promote our salvation. No words can fully express the bitterness of the sorrows which he endured; and yet he does not desire to be freed from them, till the justice of God has been satisfied, and till he has made a perfect atonement.[1]

A little later, Jesus will cry out 'It is finished' (verse 30), giving the imprimatur of God on his finished work of atonement. Now he simply says, 'I thirst.'

2. Scripture Was Being Fulfilled

John adds a second reason: it was 'to fulfil the Scripture' that Jesus said 'I thirst. The words are from Psalm 69:21. Jesus is self-consciously identifying himself with the godly sufferer in the psalm. In his unfathomable cry of forsakenness, Jesus' sense of who he was had been eclipsed. He felt he was only a suffering servant, certainly not a well-belov-

---

[1] John Calvin, commentary on John 19:28.

ed Son. But now he has come through the worst and his sense of being the Lord's suffering Servant is returning to him. Every little detail of our Lord's life was prophesied, and Jesus' whole life is self-consciously shaped by God's written word. He is uniquely *unius homo libri*, the man of one book.

Accepting the Drink

Why does Jesus now accept a drink when earlier he had refused a drink (Mark 15:23)? The reason is this: Jesus refused to have his sufferings in any way alleviated by taking a drug, a soporific that would have dulled, perhaps even deadened, his senses. He needed to be alert to the last and to be a wholly willing servant-victim. The wine mixed with myrrh would have dulled his senses. So, when the thief beside him said, 'Jesus remember me when you come into your kingdom,' Jesus was not insensitive to his prayer; he was instantly alert and said, 'Today you will be with me in Paradise' (Luke 23:42, 43).

In his dying moments Jesus also remembers to care for his mother and commends her to the apostle John's care (John 19:26, 27). He loved and served to the end. One commentator helpfully says that Jesus is never anaesthetised to the needs of his own. He not only knows, he feels our every need.

We can also say Jesus was involved in a titanic struggle with the powers of darkness. Even on the cross, the evil one was unrelenting in his temptations, 'Come down from the cross.' In this struggle unto death, the Lord needed his full mental faculties to repel Satan's suggestions.

The potential relief offered by the wine was actually a last attempt to render Jesus a mindless sacrifice. But Jesus was resolved, no matter the suffering, to experience the *process* as well as the *fact* of death. His death on the cross was not immediate or sudden. The dark, sore awfulness of death as the wages of sin, was embraced by the Sinless One. He tasted its darkness, its horror, its curse in all its unrelieved intensity. Only when the full weight of death as the wages of sin had done its worst, did Jesus then cry, 'It is finished.' Only then, as we will see, did he dismiss his spirit into the hands of his Father in full possession of all his faculties.

True Humanity

In saying 'I thirst' Jesus was expressing his true humanity. Often we are so committed to defending the true deity of Jesus (and rightly so) that we fail to give adequate emphasis to the New Testament's insistence on the Lord's true humanity. Jesus was not a divinized man, nor a humanized God. In numerous ways the Gospels underscore the true humanity of our Saviour: He ate, he slept, he grew weary, he wept. He truly was bone of our bone and flesh of our flesh. His humanity was no mere appearance of humanity; he 'became flesh' (John 1:14). Jesus' humanity was not a cloak he wore, a cloak he shed at his ascension.

He became flesh and ever will be flesh. Why is this so significant? Listen to John Calvin's fine explanation:

> It was imperative that he who was to become our Redeemer be true God and true man. It was his task to swallow up death. Who but the Life could do this? It was his task to conquer sin. Who but very Righteousness could do this? … Accordingly, our Lord came forth as true man … to present our flesh as the price of satisfaction to God's righteous judgment, and, in the same flesh, to pay the penalty that we had deserved. In short, since neither as God alone could he feel death, nor as man alone could he overcome it, he coupled human nature with divine that to atone for sin he might submit the weakness of the one to death; and that, wrestling with death by the power of the other nature, he might win victory for us.[1]

The suffering of Jesus on Calvary's cross was no pretence. His suffering was tangible, pain-filled physical suffering. There was a widespread heresy taught in the Hellenistic world that Jesus didn't really come in flesh and blood, much less die a physical death on the cross. Flesh belonged to the material realm of evil. The goal of true spirituality was to escape from the material. Only pure spirit was capable of the divine. So Jesus didn't really die, he only appeared to. This was the heresy taught by Docetism and Gnosticism. In his first letter, the apostle John wrote against this denial of the true humanity of

---

[1] *Institutes*, II.xii.2-3

Jesus: 'Every spirit that confesses that Jesus Christ has come in the flesh is from God, and every spirit that does not confess Jesus is not from God. And this is the spirit of the antichrist' (1 John 4:2, 3). 'Many deceivers, who do not acknowledge Jesus Christ as coming in the flesh, have gone out into the world. Any such person is the deceiver and the antichrist' (2 John 7).

Jesus' fifth word from the cross—'I thirst'—reminds us that Jesus died in the flesh for us and for our sins.

Jesus' Knowledge of the Scriptures

'I thirst' also reminds us of Jesus' extensive knowledge of the prophetic scriptures which foretold his suffering and death, and his willingness to fulfil each of them to the letter.

It may be appropriate to ask, How did Jesus know the Scriptures so well? At the beginning of his public ministry we find Jesus repelling the temptations of the devil by quoting three times from the book of Deuteronomy (Matt. 4:1-11). Now, as he hangs on Calvary's cross, he quotes from Psalms 22, 31, 69. How did Jesus know the Scriptures so well and so appropriately? In our discussion of the third Servant Song (Isa. 50:4-11), we saw that Jesus was not excused the educative and maturative process of human learning. Morning by morning he applied himself to knowing and understanding the word of God. Jesus' knowledge of God's word did not come to him by divine *fiat*; it came to him by mental application.

Jesus' action to ask for a drink is deliberately prompted by his knowledge of Scripture and his determination to fulfil Scripture.

The Need for Strength

Jesus said, 'I thirst' to strengthen himself and ease his throat so that he might cry out his final words from the cross 'with a loud voice.' He was summoning himself to bring it all to completion. These two little words highlight the fragility of our Saviour's humanity. There was a finitude to Jesus' human capacities. Luke tells us that in Jesus' struggle in the garden of Gethsemane 'there appeared to him an angel from heaven, strengthening him' (Luke 22:43). The Bible could not be more insistent that the humanity of the Son of God was a true humanity. Here is a Saviour who knows weakness and need from within. He has stood where we all stand. And he is therefore able to help us, as our great High Priest, in all our times of need (read Heb. 4:14-16). He knows our frame and never forgets that we are dust (Psa. 103:14).

In these two little words, we are being shown how able our Lord Jesus is to help us in the trials and troubles that touch our lives as Christians. He knows personally by experience what it is to 'thirst,' to suffer want, to be parched, to ache for help. He is not unable to sympathize with our weaknesses (the double negative strengthens the fact that he is able to help us in our weaknesses). Whatever weakness besets you, there is a Saviour who is perfectly able and willing to help you. Go to him.

CHAPTER 17

JESUS' SIXTH WORD FROM THE CROSS

John 19:30

JESUS' cry of victory, 'It is finished,' is possibly the most well known and best loved of the Saviour's words from the cross. The awful, unfathomable cry of forsakenness is followed by this cry of triumph. The ordeal is over, the powers of darkness have done their worst and been vanquished. God's eternal plan has been fulfilled. 'It is finished.'

The phrase 'It is finished' is actually just one word in the Greek text, *tetelestai*. John has just used this word in verse 28 ('knowing that all was now *finished—tetelestai*). John now wants to impress on us, from the very lips of Jesus himself, the perfect completeness of his mission.

What we need to ask is this, What is it that was 'finished' on the cross? What was the cross actually all about?

From one perspective, as we have already noted, the cross was planned by Jesus' sworn enemies. You cannot read the Gospel narratives and not be struck by the conniving of plotters, the suborning of witnesses, the wilful manipulation of the facts that conspired to put Jesus on the cross. He is where he is because wicked men determined to kill him, to remove him from the scene, to destroy Jesus' influence over the people. What these wicked yet deeply religious men had planned had come to pass. Their plot had been successful. 'It is finished.'

If we were to stop there, we would be completely blind to what C. S. Lewis called 'the deeper magic.' Jesus is where he is not because Judas betrayed him, not because the Jews hated him, not because Pilate feared him, but because the Father loved us (and loved his Son!). The cross was the deliberately planned, the eternally planned, purpose of God. He decreed it (Acts 2:23; Eph. 1:11). He was the primary actor in the drama. What Judas, the Jews, and Pilate did, they did freely, but all of their free actions were decreed within God's saving purpose to rescue sinners from the wrath to come.

Jesus came into our world as the Servant of the Lord. He came on a mission, a mission given to him by his Father (read Isa. 42:1ff.; John 6:38; 10:17). This mission had a number of strands to it.

He came to die the just for the unjust to bring us to God (1 Pet. 3:18; Matt. 1:21).

He came to bring glory to his Father (John 17:1-5).

He came to vanquish the powers of darkness (Col. 2:15; 1 John 3:8). Jesus is *Christus Victor!*

He came to become the firstborn of many brothers (Rom. 8:29). This is one of the most significant verses in the New Testament. Here we see that God's ultimate purpose is not our salvation, but the exaltation of his Son. We are God's *proximate* purpose. The exaltation of his Son is God's *ultimate* purpose.

With these truths in mind, what did Jesus mean when he cried, 'It is finished'?

Suffering Over
He meant that his own suffering was over. In just a moment Jesus will dismiss his spirit into the hands of his Father. The unimaginable pain and suffering, physical, mental and above all spiritual, was over.

Prophecies Fulfilled
He meant that all the prophesies and promises concerning him as God's suffering Servant were completed. All that was depicted in such graphic detail in the fourth Servant Song (Isa. 52:13–53:12) had come to its ordained completion.

Obedience Completed
He meant that his obedience to the Father as his sin-bearing, sin-atoning Servant had come to its completion. He had been 'obedient to the point of death, even death on a cross' (Phil. 2:8). From the moment of his conception

in the Virgin Mary's womb, Jesus had relentlessly, faithfully, and trustingly lived in obedience to his Father. Even when the shadow of the cross penetrated his human soul in the garden of Gethsemane, he said, 'Not my will but yours be done.' His eternally decreed humiliation, his willingly and lovingly embraced humiliation, was finished. Jesus is now about to enter a new phase of his mediatorial glory.

Cry of Triumph

He meant that in his expiring weakness he was triumphant. The other Gospels tell us that the cry 'It is finished' was not a whimper, it was 'loud.' How could a man so weak, so exhausted, summon up a loud piercing cry? Perhaps the writer to the Hebrews can help us answer this question. We read of Jesus in Hebrews 12:2, 'who for the joy that was set before him endured the cross, despising the shame, and is seated at the right hand of the throne of God.' Jesus' cry was a cry of anticipated glory. In his utter weakness Jesus saw the 'eternal glories' that awaited him, and summoning every last ounce of energy he cried, 'It is finished.'

Atonement Completed

In his cry Jesus meant that the awful price of making atonement for sin had been paid. Taking the place of his people he had drunk the cup of God's wrath and paid in full the ransom needed to redeem them. 'I have completed the work you gave me to do' (John 17:4). Nothing more was needed. All had been done, the work of atonement was finished. By one act of perfect obedience and sacrifice, God in Christ provided pardon and peace for everyone who will believe in Jesus. The letter to the Hebrews tells us that

> when Christ appeared as a high priest of the good things that have come, then through the greater and more perfect tent (not made with hands, that is, not of this creation) he entered once for all into the holy places, not by means of the blood of goats and calves but by means of his own blood, thus securing an eternal redemption (Heb. 9:11, 12).

'Once for all.' This is why the Roman mass is so offensive and blasphemous. The death of Jesus Christ on Calvary's cross was as unrepeatable as God's creation of the cosmos out of nothing; as unrepeatable as Jesus' incarnation; as unrepeatable as his resurrection. 'Once for all.'

Jesus' Continuing Work

When we think of the Saviour's finished work, we must keep in mind that he also has a continuing work to do. There is work to be done beyond the *tetelestai*. Our Lord Jesus is not presently existing in self-indulgent ease in heaven's glory. He is presently interceding continually for all his people at God's right hand (read Heb. 7:25 and Rom. 8:34). In the Old Testament we see that the work of a priest was both to offer sacrifices for sin and to intercede with God for the people. As our great High Priest, Jesus continues to work as our Redeemer giving eternal life to all those given to him by his Father, defending us from all our enemies, subduing and defeating the sin that yet remains to trouble us, and bringing to nothing the schemes of our great enemy, the devil.

Three Appearings

There are three phases to the work of Christ, all related to his 'three appearings':

He has appeared, in his incarnate life (Heb. 9:26b);

He 'now appears' in God's presence as our great High Priest (Heb. 9:24b);

He 'will appear' a second time in power and glory to consummate history and inaugurate the new heavens and the new earth (Heb. 9:28).

The purpose of his first coming has been completed, 'It is finished.' Now in heaven's glory he continues as our great high priest to work on our behalf. One coming day he will appear again and God will be all in all (1 Cor. 15:28).

'It is finished.' He has done it all. We can add nothing to his work. Our response is to come to him (Matt. 11:28) and receive the 'so great salvation' that he has secured for all who do so.

C. H. Spurgeon comments on Jesus' sixth word thus:

> What a grand utterance! Now are we safe, for salvation is complete. The debt was now, to the last farthing,

all discharged. The atonement and propitiation were made once and for all and forever, by the one offering made in Jesus' body on the tree. There was the cup; hell was in it; the Saviour drank it—not a sip and then a pause—not a draught [a single act of drinking] and then a ceasing. He drained it till there is not a dreg left for any of his people. The great ten-thronged whip of the Law was worn out upon his back. There is no lash left with which to smite one for whom Jesus died. The great cannonade of God's justice has exhausted all its ammunition—there is nothing left to be hurled against a child of God. [Beloved, do you believe these great benefits are yours in Christ?] Sheathed is thy sword, O Justice! Silenced is thy thunder, O Law! There remains nothing now of all the griefs and pains and agonies which chosen sinners ought to have suffered for their sins, for Christ has endured all for his own beloved and IT IS FINISHED. Christ has paid the debt which all the torments of eternity could not have paid. Once again—when he said, 'IT IS FINISHED,' Jesus had totally destroyed the power of Satan, of sin and of death. The Champion accepted the challenge to do battle for our soul's redemption against all our foes. He met Sin. Horrible, terrible, all-but omnipotent Sin nailed him to the cross. But in that deed, Christ nailed Sin also to the tree. There they both did hang together—Sin and Sin's Destroyer. Sin destroyed Christ and by that destruction Christ destroyed Sin.

CHAPTER 18

JESUS' SEVENTH WORD FROM THE CROSS

Luke 23:46

A DYING man or woman's final words are deeply significant. As John Owen, the English Puritan, lay dying, he said, to his publisher, 'O brother Payne! the long wished-for day is come at last, in which I shall see that glory in another manner than I have ever done, or was capable of doing, in this world.' The early Methodists believed that the gospel enables a person not only to live well but to die well.

It is Luke who records Jesus' final words before he expired on the cross. Luke makes no mention of the cry of forsakenness or the loud cry 'It is finished,' but he does record what are almost certainly the Saviour's last words spoken on the cross. We need the united witness of the four Gospels to begin to grasp something of the length and breadth and height and depth of God's love in Christ.

The Context

'Then the curtain of the temple was torn in two' (Luke 23:45b). The great symbol of restricted access to God has been torn asunder. The way into the holiest is now open through the blood of Jesus. The curtain had been for centuries a barrier between God's covenant people and God. Only the high priest was allowed access into the 'Holy of Holies,' and he but once a year. Now the access into God's nearer presence has been opened up for all who believe.

A Loud Cry

'Then,' not with a whisper but with a 'loud voice,' Jesus cried out, 'Father, into your hands I commit my spirit' (Luke 23:46). It is as if Jesus wanted everyone to hear that his confidence in his Father had not failed and that he was assured of his Father's acceptance. Formerly, Jesus could not speak of God as 'Father.' His filial relationship to God had been eclipsed by his sin-atoning death on the cross. But 'the price had been paid,' the sunshine of his Father's love again illumined his mind and heart. Once again the glorious word 'Father' is spoken from the Saviour's lips.

Scripture Fulfilled

Again Jesus uses one of the Psalms to express his faith as God's Servant (Psa. 31). The first thing we should notice is that Jesus changes the tense of the verb 'commit.' In

Psalm 31:5 the verb in the Hebrew is future, 'into your hands I will commit my spirit.' The psalmist prays to be saved from death, and he promises that when death eventually comes he will commit his spirit into the hands of God. But for Jesus death is not future, but imminent. He is about to expire and in his dying moment he commits his soul into the hands of his Father.

Further, we should notice that his sense of being the Father's Son had returned to him. The Father is no longer 'God,' he is '*Abba*.' It is because Jesus 'endured the cross,' bore God's wrath against our sin, was forsaken and cut off from God, that we can now say, 'Our Father.' It cost our Saviour his life, and more, to give us the glorious privilege of calling the living God our 'Father.'

While the experience of Jesus on the cross was unique, it is more than possible that believers also will at times lose the sense of God's Fatherhood. What we must never forget, is that God does not ever stop being our Father. He cannot stop being our Father. Why? Because we are united to the Son he loves. Jesus is 'the firstborn of many brothers' (Rom. 8:29), and he is not ashamed to call us his brothers (Heb. 2:11).

A Voluntary Death

In committing his spirit into the hands of his Father, Jesus used a verb, 'commit' (*paratithemi*), to highlight that he alone is in control of the timing of his death. Jesus died voluntarily. He is not like the psalmist who prayed to be delivered from death. In John 19:30, the apostle uses the same verb (*paradidomai*) that Paul uses when he speaks of God 'delivering up' his own Son to death (Rom. 8:32). Jesus delivered up his spirit at the time of his choosing. 'Death does not come till he signifies his readiness,' said Augustine. Jesus alone decided when to stop breathing. From beginning to end every event of the cross was decreed and determined by God. Augustine has this wonderful comment:

> Who can thus sleep when he pleases, as Jesus died when he pleased? Who is there that thus puts off his garment when he pleases, as he puts off his flesh at his pleasure? Who is there that thus departs when he pleases as he departed this life at his pleasure? How great the power, to be hoped for or dreaded, that must be his as Judge, if such was the power he exhibited as a dying man?[1]

The great point is that Jesus does this as the Father's obedient Servant. It is as a voluntary, willing sacrifice that he offers himself. No other sacrifice would do.

No less are Christians to devote their whole selves to God. Nothing less is worthy of the God who spared not his only Son but delivered him up for us all (Rom. 8:32). This is why Paul writes, 'I appeal to you therefore, brothers, by the mercies of God, to present your bodies as a living sacrifice, holy and acceptable to God, which is your spiritual worship' (Rom 12:1).

[1] Augustine, Homilies on John, CXIX, 6.

Jesus' second modification of the language of Psalm 31 is his use of 'Father,' as we have noted. John Calvin helpfully comments,

> Faith has no more real or solid approbation than when a godly man, seeing himself attacked on all sides, and unable to find comfort in men, despises the world's madness and unburdens on God's lap his griefs and cares, and rests quietly in the hope of his promises.[1]

However, we must say more. Because Jesus is where he is as our covenant head, representing all whom the Father gave to him (John 17:2), when he committed his spirit into his Father's hands he was committing all his people with him. We can die safely and securely because our covenant head and Saviour did. The foundational truth of our union with Christ is surely one of the most precious of truths revealed in God's word.

In his rich exposition of the glory of Christ, John Owen sees in these last words of Jesus on the cross 'the last victorious act of faith.' In this dying act of faith, the Lord Jesus Christ sets us, says Owen, a 'great example.'[2] Owen's conclusion is worth repeating:

> Now, therefore, with quietness and confidence give up thyself unto the sovereign power, grace, truth and faithfulness of God, and thou shalt find assured rest

[1] John Calvin, Commentary on Psalm 31.
[2] John Owen, 'A Declaration of the Glorious Mystery of the Person of Christ' in *Works of John Owen*, vol. 1 (London: Banner of Truth Trust, 1965), p. 280.

and peace. …Then shall he, by an act of his almighty power, not only restore thee unto thy pristine glory, as at the first creation … but enrich and adorn thee with inconceivable privileges and advantages.[1]

Seven words from the cross. The last words of a dying Saviour. In those words we are given a window into the heart and mind of Jesus as he experienced unimaginable suffering and the relentless advance of death. Here is the Holy One of God, and he is dying. Here is God's personally sinless Son and he is dying on a cross (Deut. 21:23). But listen to the words that come from his mouth:

'Father, forgive them';

'Today you will be with me in paradise';

'Woman, behold your son';

'My God, my God, why have you forsaken me?';

'I thirst';

'It is finished';

'Father, into you hands I commit my spirit.'

Here is a theology of the cross from the lips of God's own Son. It is a theology dominated by self-denying obedience, by amazing grace, by undeserved mercy, by unimaginable kindness, by prophecy fulfilled.

---

[1] *Works of John Owen*, vol. 1, pp. 281-83.

CHAPTER 19

TWO POSTSCRIPTS

Matthew 27:51-54; 27:57–28:20

AFTER Jesus finally breathed his last, something remarkable happened. Matthew records that the curtain in the temple was torn in two, that the earth shook and the rocks were split, that many bodies of the saints were raised from their tombs and appeared to many in Jerusalem, and that a hardened Roman centurion confessed Jesus to be 'the [or, a] Son of God' (Matt. 27:51-54). What are we to make of these three unexpected events?

Up until this point there has been a studied solemnity to Matthew's account of Jesus' arrest, trial, and crucifixion. But now Matthew records three supernatural happenings and the confession of a centurion, an uncovenanted Gentile, who openly acknowledged Jesus to be who he truly was.

A Torn Curtain

The curtain of the temple was torn in two. The regulations for the building of the tabernacle included the making of a curtain or veil to shut off the Holy of Holies from public view (Exod. 26:1-14). In 1 Kings 6 and 2 Chronicles 3, the dimensions of Solomon's temple lead us to believe that the curtain measured some thirty feet square. According to the Jewish historian Josephus, King Herod increased the height of the temple to nearer sixty feet. So, this was no flimsy muslin curtain. It was massive, and according to Josephus, at least two inches thick. The purpose of the curtain was to shut off the Most Holy Place and act as a barrier to everyone, with the exception of the high priest, who was allowed in behind the curtain once a year to make atonement for sin. The symbolism of the torn curtain is unmistakable. By his sin-atoning death Jesus had, in himself, opened up the way to God for sinful humanity. The writer to the Hebrews makes the point explicitly:

> Therefore, brothers, since we have confidence to enter the Most Holy Place by the blood of Jesus, by a new and living way opened for us through the curtain, that is, his body, and since we have a great priest over the house of God, let us draw near to God with a sincere heart in full assurance of faith (Heb. 10:20-22a).

The tearing of the curtain 'from top to bottom' further highlighted the miraculous, divinely sovereign nature of the tearing. The old covenant form or dispensation of the worship of God was passing away. God's new temple, his own Son, Jesus Christ (see John 2:20-21), had appeared. Access to God, acceptance with God, and the true worship of God, was now located in Christ (John 14:6).

Rocks Split

The second miraculous sign was the earth shaking and the rocks splitting. It is as if nature was recognizing the momentous nature of what has just happened. Just as there was 'darkness over all the land' (Matt. 27:45), so now nature continues to reverberate with the cosmic unfathomableness of the 'great transaction,' God in Christ becoming the sin-bearer for a world of guilty, judgment-deserving men and women.

Empty Tombs

The third miraculous sign accompanying Jesus' death must have stunned those who witnessed it. The unnatural earthquake caused tombs to open, 'and the bodies of many holy people who had died were raised to life. They came out of the tombs, and after Jesus' resurrection they went into the holy city and appeared to many people' (Matt. 27:52, 53). Just as the sun unnaturally was darkened at midday when Jesus was crucified, so now another unnatural portent signalled the epochal momentousness of the Saviour's death. It is little wonder that B. B. Warfield described the Christian faith as 'unembarrassed supernaturalism.' John Calvin helpfully explains the theological significance of this momentous and mysterious event:

> This was also a striking miracle, by which God declared that his Son entered into the prison of death, not to continue to be shut up there, but to bring out all who were held captive. For at the very time when the despicable weakness of the flesh was beheld in the person of Christ, the magnificent and divine energy of his death penetrated even to hell. This is the reason why, when he was about to be shut up in a sepulchre, other sepulchres were opened by him.

The raising of these holy people from the grave 'should be regarded as a foretoken of the Last Day, a proof that Jesus' death had in principle bought the resurrection of his people. In other words, it was an eschatological sign.'[1]

The relationship between the holy people coming out of their tombs and, after Jesus' resurrection, going into the holy city, appearing to many people, has been much discussed by commentators. Again, Calvin expresses what may be the best way to understand the text:

> Yet it is doubtful if this opening of the graves took place before his resurrection; for, in my opinion, the resurrection of the saints, which is mentioned immediately afterwards, was subsequent to the resurrection of Christ. There is no probability in the conjecture of some commentators that, after having received life and

---

[1] Herman N. Ridderbos, *Matthew: The Student's Bible Commentary* (Grand Rapids: Zondervan, 1987), p. 536.

breath, they remained three days concealed in their graves. I think it more probable that, when Christ died, the graves were immediately opened: and that, when he rose, some of the godly, having received life, went out of their graves, and were seen in the city. For Christ is called the first-born from the dead (Col. 1:18), and the first-fruits of those who rise (1 Cor. 15:20), because by his death he commenced, and by his resurrection he completed, a new life; not that, when he died, the dead were immediately raised, but because his death was the source and commencement of life. This reason, therefore, is fully applicable, since the opening of the graves was the presage [foretaste] of a new life, that the fruit or result appeared three days afterwards, because Christ, in rising from the dead, brought others along with him out of their graves as his companions. Now by this sign it was made evident, that he neither died nor rose again in a private capacity, but in order to shed the odour of life on all believers.[1]

It should not surprise us that the epochal event of the sin-atoning death of the God-Man should be accompanied by equally profound and mysterious events. This is only problematic to those who reduce God's revelation in Holy Scripture to truths that sit comfortably within the confines of human reasoning. It should always deeply impress us that after expounding the gospel of the grace of God in Christ in Romans 1:1–11:32, Paul is constrained to

---

[1] John Calvin, *Calvin's Commentaries*, vol. 17, Harmony of Matthew, Mark and Luke (Grand Rapids: Baker, 1993), pp. 324-25.

WORDS FROM THE CROSS

cry out, 'Oh, the depth' (see Rom. 11:33-36). The gospel is never irrational; but it most certainly is supra-rational. If it were not, it could not be the 'gospel of God' (Rom. 1:1).

The Firstfruit of Jesus' Death

The miraculous signs were convincing signs for the Roman centurion and those who were with him. Matthew tells us they were 'terrified,' and well they might have been as they witnessed God harnessing nature (the earthquake) and then overcoming nature (the opening of the tombs and the subsequent resurrections). What they witnessed led to the centurion's confession, 'Truly, this was the [or a] Son of God' (verse 54). It is perhaps impossible to know quite what was meant by this confession. However, in the flow of the narrative it seems more than likely that the centurion and those with him are seen by Matthew as making a gospel confession in keeping with who Jesus truly was. Each of the four Gospels were written not simply to inform and educate, but above all to persuade and convert (see Luke 1:1-4; John 20:31).

Moreover, it was an uncovenanted Gentile who was the first person to testify to Jesus' divine identity after the his death. This event anticipated the Lord's post resurrection commission to his apostles to 'go and make disciples of all nations' (Matt. 28:18-20).

The Risen and Reigning Christ

Jesus' death on the cross was simultaneously the darkest and the grandest event in human history. The holy, sinless Son of God was betrayed, denied, deserted by his friends, and brutalised and crucified by his enemies. And yet Christians call this day of all days 'Good Friday.' If Jesus' death on the cross had been the final chapter in the story we would have called that day 'Black Friday.' But the story did not end with a bloodied, nail-pierced body hanging lifeless on a Roman cross. The Old Testament prophesied that God's Messiah would rise (read Acts 13:35 which quotes Psa. 16). Jesus himself promised he would rise from the dead (Matt. 20:17-19). And now Matthew tells us that what the Old Testament prophesied and Jesus himself promised came to pass (read 1 Cor. 15:17-20).

Jesus' resurrection from the dead on the third day stands at the heart of the good news of the Christian gospel. The centrality of the resurrection is stated by Paul in Romans 4:25: Jesus 'was delivered up for our trespasses and raised for our justification.' The resurrection of Jesus was not only the public seal and vindication of his atoning work on the cross, it also secured our justification with God. Without the resurrection Jesus' work on the cross would have been a colossal failure. But 'God raised him up, loosing the pangs of death, because it was not possible for him to be held by it' (Acts 2:24).

In the concluding chapter of his Gospel, Matthew highlights both the historical fact of Jesus' resurrection,

and its theological and cosmic significance for the church
and the world.

Resurrection Joy

In Matthew 28:1-10 the evangelist recounts for us, simply
and undramatically, the risen Jesus' encounter with the
two Marys. There is no attempt to explain the mechanics
of Jesus resurrection: 'He is not here for he has risen, as
he said' (verse 6). Matthew's Gospel account began with
an angel of the Lord appearing to Joseph in a dream; and
now it all but ends with another angelic visitation. At
every significant event in Jesus' earthly life he encoun-
tered heavenly punctuations: his birth, baptism, temptations, transfiguration, Gethsemane, resurrection. I
said *at every* but there was one exception. As he hung
on Calvary's cross bearing God's just wrath against our
sin, heaven was silent. There were no punctuations, no
angelic visitations, no voices from the heavenly glory
to encourage him: 'darkness was over all the land.' But
now the price had been paid, atonement for sin had been
made, the suffering was no more. Once again, the eternal
world breaks into this present world.

What about the two Marys? The angel's words, 'Do
not be afraid' (verse 5), confront the bewilderment that
must have overtaken the two women. Can you begin to
imagine what was going though their minds—confusion, joy, bewilderment, fear? Suddenly, Jesus met them
(verses 9, 10). Their whole world was turned upside

down. Dashed hopes were replaced with evangelical joy. It is unexpected that the first post-resurrection evangelists were two fearful, joyful women! Although perhaps not so unexpected. It was Jesus' male disciples who had denied and abandoned him. Far from being tangential, the four Gospels highlight the faithfulness of the women who followed Jesus

Dark Unbelief
In Matthew 28:11-15 the evangelist breaks off his narrative to tell us about the continuing wickedness of the Jewish church leaders. Instead of calling the Gentiles to believe in the Saviour sent by God, they resisted God's work with all their might.

These ancient Jewish church leaders are little different from their modern counterparts. Modern, unbelieving churchmen are perhaps more sophisticated in their unbelief, but it is still *unbelief*. At best, Jesus is merely a good man with a kindly ethic (but an ethic that changes with the times). They refuse to bow their knees and hearts and minds before God's incarnate, crucified, risen, ascended, and reigning Son.

The King's Farewell Commission
In Matthew 28:16-20 the evangelist takes us to Galilee where Jesus meets his disciples *en masse*. We know from the other Gospels that Jesus had met with them 'on the evening of that day' (John 20:19ff.); now he meets with

them in Galilee to give them a farewell, commission. Perhaps surprisingly, Matthew tells us that 'some doubted.' Why does the evangelist tell us this? And why did some of these disciples doubt? This is yet another authentic note struck in the Gospel narrative. Jesus' followers are not unblemished. We falter and we fail. Unbelief is never far from us. But the Lord is 'rich in mercy' (Exod. 34:6, 7). The Bible never glosses over the weaknesses of even eminent believers.

It is significant that once again we find Jesus speaking to his disciples on a 'mountain' (Matt. 28:16). Jesus began his public ministry teaching on a mountain (5:1) and now as he closes his earthly mission, he returns to a mountain. Mountains are remarkably prominent throughout biblical history. It was on Mount Sinai that God gave his Ten Words to Moses (Exod. 20). It was on Mount Carmel that Elijah overcame the false prophets of Baal (1 Kings 18). It was on a mountain that Jesus delivered his 'Sermon in the Mount' (Matt. 5–7). And it was on a mountain that Jesus met Moses and Elijah and was transfigured before Peter, James, and John (Matt. 17:1-8). It is on mountains that we encounter high moments of redemptive history.

In his kingly commission, four times Jesus uses the word 'all.' Jesus is impressing on his 'little flock' the universality of his commission—universal because Jesus is the universal Lord.

As we close this study, let us consider five aspects of Jesus' regal commission.

1. An Authoritative Commission

It was an authoritative commission. The one who issues this commission has 'all authority in heaven and on earth.' Jesus is clearly echoing, and fulfilling, the words of Daniel 7:13, 14:

> I saw in the night visions, and behold, with the clouds of heaven there came one like a son of man, and he came to the Ancient of Days and was presented before him. And to him was given dominion and glory and a kingdom, that all peoples, nations, and languages should serve him; his dominion is an everlasting dominion, which shall not pass away, and his kingdom one that shall not be destroyed.

It might be asked, Did Jesus as God's Son not always have 'all authority'? Most certainly he did. Why then does he speak here about being 'given' all authority? Jesus is speaking about the 'reward' of his perfect obedience as our Mediator and Redeemer (read Phil. 2:8, 9).

2. A Universal Commission

It was a universal commission (read Gen. 12:3; Psa. 2:8). Jesus is fulfilling God's promise to Abraham that in him all the nations of the earth would be blessed.

3. An Ecclesial Commission

It was an ecclesial commission. The commission was not just to go and make disciples; these disciples were to be baptized 'into the name of the Father and the Son and the

Holy Spirit'. Baptism in the New Testament belongs to the heart of the preaching of the church. In the book of Acts, every conversion is 'completed' with baptism. Baptism was where God publicly placed his Triune name on believing sinners and initiated them into his fellowship and the fellowship of his church. The Christian life is not lived in atomised isolation; it is lived in community with other believers as part of Christ's body (read 1 Cor. 12:12-27). Christians live under the ministry and shepherding care of the men set apart by God to be under-shepherds in the flock of God (read 1 Pet. 5:1-4; Heb. 13:7, 17). Jesus' commission is in effect to plant churches—living communities of baptized believers. This is to be the goal of those who 'go.' The force of the Greek is certainly a command. Jesus is not saying, 'As you go,' but 'Go!' Every Christian is called to bear witness of Christ as they go about their daily lives. But that is not what Jesus is saying here. The church is being commanded by its King to go to all the people groups in this world with the gospel of God.[1]

---

[1] Jesus' command is often misunderstood. If Matthew had wanted to say, 'as you are going,' he would have used a present, not an aorist, participle. Actually in every instance in Matthew when the aorist participle is followed by an aorist imperative, as here, the force of the participle is a command. So here, the command 'to go' is a necessary prerequisite for fulfilling the main injunction in the sentence, 'make disciples.' Jesus is not speaking here about everyday witnessing; he is speaking about the church, his body, deliberately giving itself to 'going' to the unreached peoples of this world.

4. A Teaching Commission

It was a teaching commission. Baptised disciples were to be taught to obey everything that Christ commands. It is the primary calling of pastors to 'preach the word, [to] be ready in season and out of season; [to] reprove, rebuke, and exhort, with complete patience and teaching' (2 Tim. 4:2). Our risen Lord governs, guides, and nourishes his sheep through the ministry of his word. At the heart of that ministry will be the proclamation of 'Jesus Christ and him crucified.'

Few things are more vital to the life of the church than its being instructed, week by week, in the knowledge of person, work, and teaching of the Lord Jesus Christ.

5. A Reassuring Commission

It was a reassuring commission: 'And behold I am with you always, to the end of the age' (Acts 1:8). This is the church's confidence as we take the gospel to the ends of the earth. We do not despise an educated ministry, we encourage it. We believe that God ordinarily uses means to accomplish his saving purposes. But our confidence is in God, in the man at the Father's right hand, in the Saviour who has sent his Spirit to indwell, help, support, and lead his people.

Conclusion

We have come to the conclusion of our study. The cross was not the final goal of the incarnation of the Son of

God. His final goal was the triumph of his resurrection, the glory of his ascension, the grace of his present high priestly care of his people, at God's right hand, his coming again in glory at the end of history, and his ultimate exaltation as the firstborn of many brothers in the new creation. The cross was not the final goal, but it was the necessary cost that secured the added glory that now adorns the glorified life of our exalted Saviour and that secured for all who believe in the Lord Jesus Christ the salvation of God that is only found in him.

THE END